The Eyes of the Heart

The Eyes of the Heart

A Memoir of
the Lost and Found

Frederick Buechner

HarperOne
An Imprint of HarperCollinsPublishers

HarperOne

HarperCollins books may be purchased for educational, business, or sales promotional use. For information please write: Special Markets Department, HarperCollins Publishers, 10 East 53rd Street, New York, NY 10022.

HarperCollins Web site: http://www.harpercollins.com

HarperCollins®, ✦®, and HarperOne™ are trademarks of HarperCollins Publishers.

FIRST HARPERCOLLINS PAPERBACK EDITION PUBLISHED IN 2000

Designed by Joseph Rutt

Library of Congress Cataloging-in-Publication Data
Buechner, Frederick.
The eyes of the heart : a memoir of the lost and found /
Frederick Buechner. — 1st ed.
Includes bibliographical references.
ISBN: 978-0-06-251639-8
1. Buechner, Frederick—Friends and associates.
2. Prresbyterian clergy—United States Biography.
I Title.
BX9225.B768A3   1999
2185'.1'092—dc21   99-23089

12 RRD(H) 12

For Noah, Caroline, and Jamie
and their great-uncle
Jamie

The Eyes
of the
Heart

one

I bring Naya into the Magic Kingdom. Naya is my grandmother, my mother's mother, who died in 1961 in her ninety-
fourth year. She walks across the green library carpet and
stands at the window looking out across the stream toward my
wife's vegetable garden and the rising meadow behind it with a
dirt track running through it up into the sugar woods on the
hillside.

The Magic Kingdom is my haven and sanctuary, the place
where I do my work, the place of my dreams and of my dreaming. I originally named it the Magic Kingdom as a kind of
joke—part Disneyland, part the Land of Oz—but by now it
has become simply its name. It consists of the small room you
enter through, where the family archives are, the office, where
my desk and writing paraphernalia are, and the library, which
is by far the largest room of the three. Its walls are lined with
ceiling-high shelves except where the windows are, and it is

divided roughly in half by shoulder-high shelves that jut out at right angles from the others but with an eight-foot space between them so that it is still one long room despite the dividers. There are such wonderful books in it that I expect people to tremble with excitement, as I would, on entering it for the first time, but few of them do so because they don't know or care enough about books to have any idea what they are seeing.

They are the books I have been collecting all my life, beginning with the Uncle Wiggily series by Howard R. Garis. In 1932, when I was six, I sent my unfortunate mother all over Washington, D.C., looking for *Uncle Wiggily's Ice Cream Party*, but she never found it, and it wasn't until about sixty years later that I finally located a copy and completed the set. There are first editions of all the Oz books, some of them the same copies I read as a child, with "Frebby Buechner" scrawled in them because I was less sure about the difference between *b*'s and *d*'s in those days than I have become since, and also of both *Alice in Wonderland* and *Alice Through the Looking Glass*, with a later edition of each signed by the original Alice herself when she came to this country in 1932 as an old lady to receive an honorary doctorate from Columbia University on the centenary of Lewis Carroll's birth. Underneath her academic robes she wore a corsage of roses and lilies of the valley and in her acceptance speech said she would prize the honor "for the rest of my days, which may not be very long." She died in 1934 at the age of eighty-two. There is a drab little Jenny Wren of Dickens's *A Christmas Carol* as first published in 1843 with green endpapers and the four hand-colored, steel-engraved plates by John

Leech, and a *Moby Dick or The Whale* in the original shabby purple-brown cloth with the "usual moderate foxing" through-out, as the catalogue description apologetically notes. There are a number of seventeenth-century folios, including the sermons of Lancelot Andrewes, Jeremy Taylor, and John Donne, that I started buying when my wife and I were on our honeymoon in England in 1956 with some British royalties that were due me then. There is North's *Plutarch* and Florio's *Montaigne* and the first collected edition of Ben Jonson, 1692, which I was beside myself with excitement to discover bore the inscription *Jo: Swift, Coll Nova* in an eighteenth-century hand, only to learn from the British Museum years later that it was not, as I'd wildly hoped, the great Jonathan but one John Swift, who matriculated at New College, Oxford, at the age of fifteen.

On the walls are the framed autographs of some of my heroes. There is a photograph of the portrait of Henry James that his friend Sargent painted on the occasion of his seventieth birthday, inscribed by both Sargent and the Master himself, who distributed prints of it to the faithful. Nearby Anthony Trollope has signed his name together with the words "Very faithfully" beneath a *carte de visite* photograph that shows him in granny glasses scowling through whiskers that erupt from his face like the stuffing of an old sofa—"all gobble and glare," as Henry James once described him in a letter—and there is a sepia cabinet photograph of Mark Twain on the lower margin of which he has written, "It is your human environment that makes climate," whatever exactly he meant by that. And then, matted with red damask in a gilt frame, there is the upper part of a sixteenth-century vellum document in which Queen Elizabeth, the only *real* Queen Elizabeth, grants permission to someone whose name I cannot make out to travel to Flanders on official business. When the trip was completed, the document was canceled with four gill-like incisions, and at the top of the page the queen signed it "Elizabeth R." Between her signature and the document's first line there are two free-floating squiggles, which my wife and I long ago decided mark where she tried out her quill pen to make sure it wouldn't spatter ink when she made the great flowing loops that fly out like pennants in the wind from the bottom of the *E* and *Z* and *R* and the upper staff of the *B*.

On the sash of the large window at the end of the room, where Naya stands waiting for me to get on with my description, there is a stone I found wedged into a crack in the rocky ledge we stepped ashore on when I made a pilgrimage to the island of Outer Farne in the North Sea one summer in honor of St. Godric, who often visited there in his seafaring days in the twelfth century and about whom I had written a novel several years earlier. In the novel I describe how on his first visit to the island Godric ran into St. Cuthbert, who had died some four hundred years before. Cuthbert says that long before Godric arrived, he was expected there and then explains himself by saying, "When a man leaves home, he leaves behind some scrap of his heart. Is it not so, Godric? . . . It's the same with a place a man is going to. Only then he sends a scrap of his heart ahead." When I finally managed to pry the stone loose with my pocketknife, I discovered, to my wonderment, that it was unmistakably heart-shaped, and I have fastened Cuthbert's explanation to the back of it with Scotch tape. On top of one of the divider bookshelves is a Rogers Group that depicts King Lear awakening from his madness in the presence of his old friend Kent, disguised as a servant, and the Doctor, and Cordelia, whose forehead he is reaching out to touch as he says, in the words inscribed on the statue's base, "You are a spirit, I know. When did you die?" On the windowsill stands the bronze head of my childhood friend, the poet James Merrill, sculpted in the summer of 1948, when we shared a house on Georgetown Island in Maine while he worked on his *First Poems* and I on *A Long Day's Dying*, which was my first novel. I remember feeling rather miffed that it was Jimmy rather than I whom our friend Morris Levine had chosen to immortalize, but I got over it.

Naya is sitting in the wing chair by the window looking as she did when she was in her late eighties. Her "eyes mid many wrinkles, her eyes," her "ancient, glittering eyes, are gay," as Yeats wrote of the old Chinamen in "Lapis Lazuli." Her hair is in a loose bun held together by several tortoise-shell pins, and there are a few stray wisps floating free. She is wearing a black dress with a diamond bar pin. One hand extends out over the arm of the chair, palm upward, and she lightly rubs her thumb and middle finger together with a circular motion, as she often did when she was waiting for something to happen.

"Jimmy was a spirit I knew," she says. "When did he die?"

He died on February 6, 1995, and on the day before, from a hospital in Arizona, he apparently made three phone calls—

one to his mother, one to his former psychiatrist, Dr. Detre, and one to me. He was having some difficulty breathing, but otherwise sounded entirely himself. He said he was glad that whatever was happening to him was happening far from home where he wouldn't be "smothered with concern," as he put it. He said that he was in no serious pain and that when they had given him some Welch's grape juice sorbet earlier in the day, it had tasted so good to him he had asked for another. He asked me to stay in touch with his mother and sent his love to my wife. I told him I would say some powerful prayers for him, and he said, "That is exactly what I want you to do." He called me "my dearest friend," which I couldn't remember his ever having done before, and when I phoned the next morning to find out how things were going with him, I was told that he had died a few hours earlier. It was only then that I realized that the purpose of his call had of course been to say good-bye, and ever since then the ground I stand on has felt less sure and solid beneath my feet.

"The poor lad," Naya says. "I remember how he used to come spend weekend passes with us in Tryon when he was in basic training at Camp Croft during the war. He sometimes played Mozart for us on that awful upright that came with the dark little cabin we were renting that year, his glasses perpetually sliding down the bridge of his nose. We talked about Proust and Elinor Wylie, and your Uncle George Wick listened to him as though he was a visitor from Mars and plied him with daiquiris till he couldn't see straight. Was there ever anybody *en ce bas monde* who was less cut out to be a GI?"

"He wrote me about a terrible march he was on once during infantry training," I tell her. "It was blistering hot, and they were all loaded down with full field packs and steel helmets and bayonets fixed to their M-I rifles. There was a grubby-faced little girl standing barefoot by the side of the red-clay road to watch, and he said that as he passed by in front of her, she handed him a peach and he burst into tears."

Naya takes a Chesterfield out of her knitting bag and places it dead center between her lips. I had forgotten all about her formidable Zippo lighter until she opens it with a metallic clink and produces a raw whiff of lighter fluid and a towering flame. Skeins of smoke drift around her head in the sunlit air as she recites, "I did but see her passing by, yet will I love her till I die."

"Can you really be there, my dearest dear, or am I only dreaming you?" I say. She narrows her eyes at me, smiling faintly, and gives me her riverboat-gambler look.

Behind her, near Jimmy's head, stand a number of framed photographs. There is my mother as a little girl of nine or ten or so in a frilly white dress and a preposterous white picture hat. Her ankles are crossed, and she is holding a spray of white flowers upside down in her lap. There is my grandfather Buechner, looking as old as time though he died when he was some three years younger than I am now. He has a pipe between his teeth and is standing in a driveway somewhere leaning on his cane. He is wearing a fedora and a velvet-collared topcoat that reaches almost to his ankles. You can dimly make out the massive figure of my grandmother Buechner brooding in the back seat of a Gothic-looking automobile parked just behind him. There is my grandfather Kuhn, Naya's husband, sitting on the deck of an ocean liner with his legs crossed and looking slender and elegant in his straw boater and stiff white collar. Not far away, on the wall of my office, there is a photograph of my father in bathing trunks and top kneeling on the sandy beach of Quogue, Long Island. He is about twenty-nine years old. In front of him, between his thighs, stands a chubby, tow-headed one year old, who is me. My father's right hand is spread out against my chest to prevent me from collapsing, and he is holding his left hand off to the side a little to keep the smoke of his cigarette out of the way. We are both looking very grave. On my birthday not long ago my youngest daughter, Sharmy, gave me a picture taken of her and her small son Benjamin on the same beach, in the same pose, and when I suddenly realized what it was, I covered my face with my hands.

The answer to my question is that yes, Naya can really be there. I suspect there is no one on earth, or anywhere else, who cannot really be there if I want them to be and summon them properly.

"I think about dying a lot these days," I say to her. "I think about how much time I've got left. Sometimes they're sad thoughts, but not always. Sometimes the sadness is lost in wondering what will come next. If anything comes."

I suppose Jimmy's death is part of it. Every month or so I dream about him. We are always saying some sort of awkward good-bye to each other, and the meetings are never very satisfactory. And of course part of it too is that I have turned seventy and have six small grandsons and one even smaller granddaughter, all of them under the age of five. Whenever I'm with them, I wonder how much of their lives I will be around to witness. Their going to school for the first time? Their first long pants? When Benjamin was born, his father asked some of us to write him letters to be read on his twenty-first birthday on August 25, 2015, which happens to fall on a Tuesday. Is it possible that at age eighty-nine I will still be around to hear mine read aloud along with the others over the crêpes suzettes and coffee, to bumble my way through some kind of grandfatherly toast? It is possible. Naya and my mother both made it into their nineties, after all. My health is good. I am a moderate drinker and haven't smoked a pipe for a long time. Will I at least be around long enough for Ben or any of them to remember me? How I carried Oliver on my shoulders some two or three miles of woodland path along the turbulent Landquart River from Klosters to Garfiun with the Swiss Alps glittering above us in the summer sun? How every time I asked Dylan, "Are you my sweet potato?" he dutifully showed his one dimple and answered "Yup" or maybe didn't answer at all, and taught his brother, Tristan, that whenever I burped in his presence, he was the one who was supposed to say "Excuse me"?

Wheeling my cart around the aisles of the Grand Union supermarket, which is my club, my Metropolitan Museum, my church, I run into people I know—some of them friends, some of them the merest acquaintances—and wonder if any of them will show up at my funeral when the day comes and how they will feel about it if they do, even where they will go on to dinner afterwards (will they change out of their church clothes first?) and what they will find to say about me there if they say anything about me at all. I look at them thinking that they too will someday reach the last of their days, maybe before I reach mine, or maybe long afterwards. I wonder what will happen, when I die, to all the marvelous books I've been collecting all my life, because none of my children seems to have any particular interest in them, and to all the old family letters and documents and photographs I have amassed and filed away in the little entrance room along with the diaries I have kept for the past forty years or so with their relentless and nearly illegible account of where we went and who went with us and what we did when we got there. Should I leave them to Wheaton College, which has most of my other papers and manuscripts, or to my children in the unlikely event that they should ever be interested? Will our two dachshunds, Otto the Importunate and his uncle, Klaus the Long-suffering, last me out, or will I be good for one more pair to replace them, conceivably even a pair after that? Will I ever see the Holy Land, or finally get around to reading *Gone with the Wind,* or learn to play golf when I get too old for tennis? Will this book I am writing be my last book?

They don't feel like morbid thoughts as I think them, but more like the kind of thoughts you have about a trip you plan to take at some undetermined time to a place you have never been. What will you take with you and what will you leave behind? When will you set off? Will you have everything more or less in order and be ready when the time comes? I think about the friends who have set off before me rather the way I remember thinking about the friends in school who graduated before me and moved on into a world I could hardly imagine. There is even a kind of dim excitement at the prospect. In no sense do I want to hasten the day, but if someone were to tell me that it is to be postponed indefinitely, I suspect that at least part of what I would feel would be a faint disappointment.

I am a hopelessly religious person, but there is nothing particularly religious about these thoughts. The time I went at his request to see my old friend and former Exeter colleague Richard Niebling when he was dying a few years ago, I asked him what he thought about the mystery that awaited him, and in an abrupt, almost irritated way, almost as if the question was too foolish to answer, he said, "I am a believer. I believe I will see God," and let it go at that. I can imagine answering it in much the same way and for the reason that, like him perhaps, it is not my ultimate destination that preoccupies me at this point so much as it is the nature of the departure—the great deep-throated blast of the liner as she starts to pull away from the pier, the wheeling gulls overhead, the first glimpse, out beyond Ellis Island and the Statue of Liberty, of the open sea.

Naya is knitting a sock and has her knitting face on—her eyebrows slightly raised, her lips pressed tight.

"You've already set sail," I say. "What can you tell me about it?"

She glances at me over the top of her spectacles and lets her needles come to rest.

"My poor, ignorant boy," she says, "don't you know better than to ask a question like that when I'm turning a heel?"

The ball of wool falls off her lap and rolls toward me across the green carpet. I pick it up and put it on her lap again.

She says, "When somebody once asked your Uncle Jim if some friend or other had passed away, he answered in his inimitable fashion by saying, 'Passed away? Good God, he's dead,' and I know just how he felt. I always thought 'passed away' was a silly way of putting it, like calling the water closet a powder room—or calling it a water closet for that matter—and I am here to tell you that it is also very misleading."

She says, "It is the *world* that passes away," and flutters one hand delicately through the air to show the manner of its passing. Her sapphire ring glitters in the sun.

"When I used to lie there in that shadowy little room Mrs. Royal gave me in her establishment that looked out onto the garden, with your blessed mother or Ruth dropping by every day or so to keep me abreast of the local gossip at Missildine's, where everybody used to congregate for a Coke after picking up the mail and Miss Capps would read the picture postcards over your shoulder, I could feel the world gradually slowing down more and more until one night, after that charming nurse whose name I regret to say I've forgotten turned out the light and was getting ready to go home, I realized it was finally slow enough for me to get off, and that is just what I proceeded to do. It was rather like getting off a streetcar before it has quite come to a stop—a little jolt when my foot first struck the pavement, and then the world clanged its bell and went rattling off down the tracks without me. Myrtle, that was her name unfortunately, but what a comfort she was."

She closes her eyes and is silent while she tries to summon up the scrap of poetry she is after. Then with one slender finger she taps out the meter on the arm of her chair as she recites it with her eyes still closed.

> *"And when, O Saki, you shall pass*
> *Among the guests star-scattered on the grass,*
> *And in your joyous errand reach the spot*
> *Where I made one, turn down an empty glass.*

"A lovely, sad thought," she says, "but for me there really wasn't any sadness. I felt nothing so much as astonishment. I had lived so many years by then that I was sure the only thing that could ever finish me off would be a violent death of some kind—a smashup on that corkscrew road to Asheville perhaps or a bolt of lightning. So then when it finally happened right there in my bed with the night light on and that nice nurse standing by, nothing could have been more peaceful, and I was astonished."

"I was sitting upstairs at my desk in Exeter when I got the news," I say, "and I remember leaning forward and resting my head on top of the typewriter and seeing my tears trickle down into the keys."

"That was a fitting tribute from a young man of literary aspirations," she says.

I say, "That was almost forty years ago, and I doubt if a single day has gone by without my missing you."

"Ours was a marriage made in Heaven," she says. "I loved to talk, and you loved to listen. Even when you were a little boy in a red beret, you would sit there with your eyes round as saucers while I rattled on."

"Tell me about wherever you are now," I say. "Rattle on about what it's like to be dead."

My mother, the elder of Naya's two daughters, refused to talk about death the way she refused to talk about a great many other things. I remember telling her once that unless she started balancing her checkbook, she would go on overdrawing her account with disastrous results for the rest of eternity, and before I had much more than begun my lecture, she clapped her hands over her ears so she couldn't hear a syllable. She refused even to talk about people she loved who had died—Naya, for instance. It made her too sad, she said. Her New York apartment was full of photographs in silver frames, leather frames, Victorian rhinestone and millefiori frames, but they were photographs only of the living. Once in Vermont when I showed her a picture that I had dug up somewhere of her father as a young man, she hardly so much as glanced at it.

But there was one day, I remember, when in the midst of some conversation we were having about nothing in particular she suddenly turned to me and said out of the blue, "Do you really believe anything *happens* after you die?" and all at once she was present to me in a way she rarely was. She was no longer onstage. She was no longer in character. She had stepped off into the wings for a moment, and the words she had spoken

14

were not in the script. Her face was for the moment not the one she had skillfully assembled in front of her dressing-table mirror that morning with lipstick, powder, and eyebrow pencil, but her own true face.

She had come a long way from the little girl in frilly white with the upside-down flowers in her lap. She was in her eighties with bad arthritis in her knees and was wearing whichever one of her many hearing aids she happened to have chosen that day, although none of them ever seemed to do her much good. I always suspected that it was not so much because she was deaf that she couldn't hear, but because there was so much she didn't want to hear that she chose to be deaf. To get anything through to her you had to say it at the top of your lungs, so in answer to her question, I said YES. I said I believed SOME-THING HAPPENS. But there are things that cannot be shouted, and as soon as I tried in my more or less normal voice to tell her a little more about what I believed and why I believed it, I could see that she was not only not hearing, but also not listening. Just to have asked the question seemed for the time being to be as much as she could handle.

So later, when I got home, I tried to answer the question in a letter. I wrote her I believe that what happens when you die is that, in ways I knew no more about than she did, you are given back your life again, and I said there were three reasons why I believed it. First, I wrote her, I believed it because, if I were God and loved the people I created and wanted them to become at last the best they had it in them to be, I couldn't imagine consigning them to oblivion when their time came with the job under the best of circumstances only a fraction done. Second, I said, I believed it, apart from any religious considerations, because I had a hunch it was true. I intuited it. I said that if the victims and the victimizers, the wise and the foolish, the good-hearted and the heartless all end up alike in the grave and that is the end of it, then life would be a black comedy, and to me, even at its worst, life doesn't *feel* like a black comedy. It feels like a mystery. It feels as though, at the innermost heart of it, there is Holiness, and that we experience all the horrors that go on both around us and within us *as* horrors rather than as just the way the cookie crumbles because, in our own innermost hearts, we belong to Holiness, which they are a tragic departure from. And lastly, I wrote her, I believe that what happens to us after we die is that we aren't dead forever because Jesus said so.

Jesus was another of the dead people I knew my mother wouldn't want to talk about, and I had no idea how she would react to my invoking his authority. I said that, because in one way Jesus was a human being like the rest of us, I imagined he could be wrong about lots of things like the rest of us too and probably believed the world was flat just the way everybody else did in his day. But when he said to the Good Thief on the cross next to his, "Today shalt thou be with me in Paradise," I wrote her, I would bet my bottom dollar that he of all people knew what he was talking about, because if in one way he was a human being, in another way he was immeasurably more.

I could hardly conceive of a more unlikely person than my mother to have written such a letter to, but since trying to shout it all to her instead was unthinkable, I mailed it anyway, and when I asked about it some weeks later, her only answer was to say that it had made her cry. I don't think that it was anything I said that made her cry; in fact I doubt if she even read my letter all the way through. I think that it was being reminded by the letter of her original question about death. I think her tears had to do with what she saw as the pathos of simply having asked it when she knew without ever talking about it that her own death couldn't be all that far away.

The only time I can remember *seeing* her cry was sometime during her late fifties when she had to have most of her upper teeth pulled and, on returning from the ordeal, threw herself face down on her bed, where for an hour or more she sobbed her heart out over what she must have felt was the end of the world. If she cried when my father committed suicide in 1936, when he was thirty-eight and she was forty, I never saw her do it; nor on the rare occasions when she talked about him during the half century and more that she survived him did I ever sense that behind her words there were tears that she was holding back. The sadness of other people's lives, even the people she loved, never seemed to touch her where she lived. I don't know why. It wasn't that she had a hard heart, I think—in many ways she was warm, sympathetic, generous—but that she had a heart that for one reason or another she kept permanently closed to other people's suffering, as well as to the darkest corners of her own.

Why not bring her, like Naya, to my Magic Kingdom to ask her about it? I think that more than anything else it is because I am afraid. I am afraid of what she might say. I am afraid of what I might say. I am afraid of her.

In an earlier memoir called *Telling Secrets*, which I delivered first as a series of three lectures before an audience some thousand strong in the ballroom of a New York hotel, I told a number of secrets about her and about my complex feelings about her. Not daring to do it while she was still alive, I gave as honest a picture of her as I knew how. I described the New York apartment where she lived the last thirty years or so of her life and the room in it where just short of ninety-two she died——her dressing table laden with beauty preparations and gadgets, the patent medicines on the bureau, the chaise longue with the fake leopard-skin throw and dozens of little pillows, the beaded Victorian pincushions, the movie magazines. I told about what I always felt was the curse upon her of having been born blue-eyed and beautiful, with the result that she never had to be especially kind and loving in order to draw people to her because they were drawn to her anyway. I told about my father and his death and a little about her marriage to him. They weren't very many or very terrible, these secrets I told about her, but they were all of them secrets that for almost a century she had kept not only from the world, but much of the time from herself, and as I stood up there at the lectern spilling them out to that huge room full of strangers, I felt sure that if she happened to turn up with a gun in her hands, she would shoot me dead without turning a hair.

I saw her for the last time a couple of months before she died. She was sitting up in bed. She had let her hair go whiter than I had ever seen it before and was wearing almost no makeup. She was looking not at me as she spoke, but down at her covers, and her words were mainly about her various aches and pains, her sleepless nights, her burning feet, the red patch that appeared on her cheek every morning and that she had to spend hours working at with face powder and cold cream to conceal. *Agony* was the word she used to describe it all, which I took to be a characteristic exaggeration. She excoriated the woman who came to stay with her nights for not giving her the bourbon and Valium she asked for to help her sleep. She excoriated my brother for his barbaric neglect. When I pointed out that the night woman was only following the doctor's orders and that she had no more devoted slave in the world than my brother, she was furious. I was totally unsympathetic as usual, she said. I never took her side in anything. "Why do you hate me?" she asked, and when I protested that if I hated her, I would not have come all the way down from Vermont to see her, she said that, simply in order to cause her pain, I had refused to stop so she could go to the bathroom the last time I had driven back from Vermont with her. Suddenly I found myself storming out of her room so full of anger that I might never have gone back, and that would have been the dismal way our last encounter ended. Even as I was going, I saw a queer look of satisfaction on her face. She had gotten a rise out of me. She had goaded me into demonstrating the very hate I had just finished denying.

But then some good angel gave me pause. She was old. She was falling to pieces. Her world was falling to pieces. Maybe agony was closer to the truth of it than I supposed. So I went back after a few moments, and neither of us made any mention of what had just taken place. We talked for a while. Her tiny doctor appeared and bound up one arthritic knee swollen to the size of a melon. And then, as I was finally leaving, she said to me, "You have always been my hero."

"Why do you hate me?" and "You have always been my hero." Those were the last two things I can remember her ever having said to me face to face.

"Why do you tell all these intimate things?" I hear her ask now. Her tone is not accusatory this time. It is hushed, intimate.

"So I can forget them?" I say. "To put them on record so they will never be forgotten?"

"You didn't cry into your typewriter when you heard I'd died," she says.

"I cried when we buried your ashes."

My brother and my wife and I had taken them out in a cardboard box to Irwin, Pennsylvania, near Pittsburgh, where we buried them in the Long Run Cemetery next to Naya and my grandfather and other Kuhn forebears going back to the eighteenth century. Over her grave I had read the passage from Revelation that describes the holy city with its walls of sapphire, emerald, topaz, and its twelve gates of pearl because she had always loved pretty things, and then as I was saying the benediction I suddenly found myself choked by a wrenching yelp of whatever it was a yelp of—grief, regret, divine relief. Unutterable love.

"That cheap little pot of ferns you left at my grave from the supermarket across the street," she says.

"It was all they had," I say. "We laughed to think what you'd have said if you knew."

"I'll bet you did," she says.

The Magic Kingdom is magically still. Naya has left her knitting in the wing chair and is standing by the window looking out. She has one finger on the glass pane.

"You ask me to rattle on about death," she says. "That is like my asking you to rattle on about life. Where would you begin? Where would you end? What could you compare life to when life is all you know?

"In life you *move forward*. That is what life is all about. 'Leg over leg the dog went to Dover,' as your grandfather was fond of quoting at the drop of a hat. From Pittsburgh we went leg over leg to Saranac the winter Ruth had trouble with her lungs and stayed there through spring despite the bitter recriminations of your mother, who had her heart set on graduating from Miss Mitchell's with her class so she could go marching down the aisle of Calvary Church with a bunch of long-stemmed roses in her arms. When we didn't spend the whole summer in Machiasport, we would often go to Saint-Jean-de-Luz or Thun, almost always ending up in Geneva to see Tante Elise Golay, who lived up in the old part of the city under the shadow of Calvin's grim cathedral with a cherry tree in her yard that had a bell in it which she could pull with a string to frighten the birds away. After your poor father died, I went to

Bermuda with your mother and you boys to help you get settled there, and what a fairy tale of an island it was in those days, with the silvery bells of the bicycles and the narrow little railway and the horses and carriages if you were feeling grand and thought you could raise the price and those dear little pink and blue cottages with their white roofs like cupcakes. To be alive is to keep moving on and on like that, even if it's only upstairs to bed at night or down to Trade Street to get that nice young Mr. Landrum to cash your meager check for you at the bank, or maybe just to see the sights like Mrs. E. Scruggs Brown, O wondrous name, in her fur piece or old C. J. Lynch, the real estate tycoon, with his extraordinary nose, standing in a doorway tipping his straw hat to all the ladies.

"And to be alive is of course always to keep moving through time too, as day follows day follows day like circus elephants holding each other's tails. You move from one time to another time to another time until finally your time runs out. That is what life is all about. But you asked me about death."

There is not much snow on the ground outside the window, but there is enough to leave it mostly white. The meadow and wooded hill beyond are lost in the November mist. Naya has one hand on her hip as she gazes out at it. There is a knitting needle stuck into her grey bun.

"Once you've stepped off the streetcar," she says, "you don't keep moving on in the same way. It's more like moving *in*—not the dog going leg over leg to Dover anymore, but instead somebody like Mr. Edison moving closer and closer to some new discovery, some revelation that will open up a whole new world, a whole new way of understanding everything. Or so you hope. I'm sorry I make it sound so uninteresting. It is really very interesting indeed."

"You make it sound lonely," I say. "Do you ever see people you used to know, people you loved?"

"My dear boy," she says. "Words like *see* don't do very well on this side of things. But yes, they are here. They are part of what, ever so slowly, we move deeper and deeper toward, or into, or through—whatever the preposition is. They are part of what we begin little by little to understand at last."

I almost don't dare to ask it, but then I do. "Is Daddy there?"

"They all are," she says.

It has been more than sixty years since that early morning in New Jersey when I saw him last, and although I remember a few isolated things about him, my father himself I can't remember. I can't remember his face or his voice. I can't remember loving him. I can't even remember remembering him.

But I do not ask Naya now to tell me whatever she can about where he is or how he is or who he is. And to bring him back now to this peaceful room full of books would be unthinkable. The reason, I think, is fear.

It is fear that keeps me from bringing my mother back, and it is fear also, I think, that keeps me from bringing my father back, although a different kind of fear. I do not bring my mother back for fear that she will be too much for me. Maybe I do not bring my father back for fear that he will be too little. Or that I will be. I suppose one way to read my whole life—my religious faith, the books I have written, the friends I have made—is as a search for him. Maybe at its heart my fear is the fear of finding him.

Whenever I used to meet people who had known him, I would ask them to tell me what he was like, and they would always say more or less the same thing. He was charming, handsome, a good athlete, a good dancer. He was kind. Everybody liked him. It was the standard response, and I'm sure it was true, but it was not what I was after. It gave me no sense of what it felt like to be with him, the kind of things he laughed at or that made him mad, the look in his eye, the kind of neckties he wore. It was my daughter Katherine who told me once that the trouble was that I was asking it the wrong way. "What was he like?" was too big a question, she said. It scared people off. If you want to get a big answer, she said, you should ask a little question. I should ask people if they remembered ever eating a meal with him. Or playing tennis with him. Or arguing with him about politics. Or being with him at a bar, or the movies, or on a subway. Who could say what one small, concrete memory might jog loose?

Not long afterwards, I ran into a man in his nineties who had been in his class at Princeton. His name was Ed Pulling, former headmaster of the Millbrook School, and when I did as I had been told and asked if he could remember anything specific and concrete about him—some scene, some moment, some glimpse—I could see that he was giving the matter serious thought. After a while he said that nothing seemed to come to his mind of the sort I was after, but he promised that he would go on thinking about it and would write me if anything occurred to him. What's more, he said, there were a few other members of the class still around, and he would get in touch with them and see what they might be able to dig up. To my surprise, he remembered his promise, and after a month or so wrote to say that unfortunately neither he nor any of the others he had talked to had been able to come up with a thing. So many years had gone by. So many memories had faded. He was sorry and wished me well on my search.

My father had been a charming, handsome young man, he said, and everybody had liked him.

two

Standing upright on the mantel is a tray my old friend John Kouwenhoven gave me one Christmas, having painstakingly pasted on it and varnished some forty-eight covers of Between the Acts and Bravo cigarette boxes (Thos. H. Hall, Manufacturers, N.Y.) that he must have collected for years. They date from the last decades of the nineteenth century and bear the lithographed head-and-shoulder likenesses of some of the leading theatrical lights of the day. Mr. M. Arbuckle is among them, wearing a braided uniform of some kind and glowering out of a Napoleon III beard and moustache with just enough of a double chin in evidence to make you wonder if he could possibly have been a kinsman of the immortal Fatty. A few covers to the right of him is E. L. Davenport in the role of Brutus, looking both very fierce and a little inebriated with his hair in disarray and a toga that he seems to have slipped on backwards. In a row above, plump Miss E. Somerville simpers

27

under the wide, round brim of a hat with pompoms dangling from it. She has squeezed herself into a low-cut bodice and has raised one hand flirtatiously in front of the lower part of her face, the fingers artfully arranged as if to pick something, possibly edible, out of the air. Several of these luminaries were apparently so famous in their time that a single name sufficed to identify them—like Sonnenthal, who has bangs, false teeth, and a wing collar, and a formidable woman billed simply as Materna in what seem to be widow's weeds and a pleated black bonnet the shape of an inverted coal scuttle.

Near the tray is a tall, ink-blue Staffordshire cup with a gold handle and the monogram "EviiiR" underneath a gold crown. It was turned out as a souvenir of Edward VIII's accession to the throne and bought by my mother in Bermuda in 1937 because she thought it might be worth something someday, as for all I know it is. On the other side of the tray from the cup is a man's gold pocket watch hanging inside a glass bell jar. It was my father's watch and has his initials engraved on the back—C.F.B., the same as mine. In the three or four lines he wrote my mother in pencil on the last page of *Gone with the Wind*, which she was reading at the time because it had just come out and was all the rage, he asked her to give the watch to me and his pearl stickpin to my brother, Jamie, because those two things were virtually all that he had in his possession to give anybody. By leaving his note where he did, I have always assumed he hoped that only she would ever see it and thus no one else would need to know the way he died, which of course everybody did anyway. "Give Freddy my watch. Give

Jamie my pearl pin. I give you all my love," he wrote, and for years I have wondered whether the "all" goes with "you" or with "my love." Did he mean that he gave all his love to my mother or that he gave it to all three of us to divide among us as best we could? He signed it "Your Fred" and then added four unsteady, lopsided X's, the last of which is almost too faint to see.

At the far left end of the mantel is the life-size hand of a Ceylonese Buddha broken off just above the wrist and mounted on a wooden base skillfully cut to fit the jagged end. Made of bronze with traces of the original gilt still visible in places, it is the Buddha's right hand raised as if in blessing with the thumb and fingers standing tight together as tall and slender as saplings. Jimmy Merrill gave it to me on what turned out to be our last meeting, not counting the harried glimpse we had of each other one evening as my wife and I were hurrying to the theater several months later and happened upon him standing with a friend under the marquee of *Sunset Boulevard*, whose music, he wrote me afterwards, struck him as "of terminal insipidity."

Our last real meeting took place in his apartment, which I had known first in 1940 when we were both fourteen and it had belonged to his Ingram grandmother, known by everybody as Mis' Annie, a little wry-faced firecracker of a woman from Fernandina, Florida, with a cracked voice and long red fingernails, who at one point had in her employ a Father Divine convert named Love Joy, whose services came to a dramatic end the morning she brought in the breakfast tray with the news that there was blood flowing out of the carpet sweeper. Jimmy hadn't been well that winter—it was in May that we met in Mis' Annie's apartment—and though he said that he was feeling much better, I thought he looked a little precarious. We talked about his health for a while, how there had been moments when he thought he was "slipping through the cracks," as he put it, and when I asked if he had written anything about it he read me a poem he had done about a visit to the doctor who had shown him the color photograph of a blood slide, which the poem describes as a Christmas tree with "Chains of gold tinsel, baubles of green fire / For the arterial branching," and then goes on to say,

> Defenseless, the patrician cells await
> Invasion by the barbaric viruses,
> Another sack of Rome.
> A new age. Everything we dread.

and ends with the lines:

> Dread? It crows for joy in the manger.
> Joy? The tree sparkles on which it will die.

I was so moved by Jimmy's reading of it that when he finished, I reached out and touched his hand. Although he gave no visible sign of it because that was not his style, I thought I could tell that he also was moved, but the subject was too charged to pursue any further, and we turned quickly to other matters. He told me I should read Georges Perec's marvelously lunatic *Life, a User's Manual,* and I recommended to him Annie Dillard's *Holy the Firm,* and then we went out for a lunch of soup at a nearby deli and on the corner of 72nd Street and Lexington Avenue embraced like elderly saints in a Giotto fresco and said good-bye for the last time.

I have had many dreams about him since his death—unsatisfactory, shadowy encounters for the most part, usually in some cluttered setting like a museum, or a railway station, or a cocktail party—and it is always good-bye that we are saying again as if to make up for never having had the chance to say it properly and conclusively, knowing that it was for the last time the way my father did when he penciled his note with the four wobbly X's. Or maybe what the dreams reflect is that, although in an almost ceremonial way we remained each other's "dearest friend" for all those decades, our lives had long since led us down such different paths that in a sense we had said good-bye many years before—Jimmy gay, a poet, an intellectual, a citizen of the world, and I straight, a minister (of all things), bookish, and for some forty years or so a citizen of Rupert, Vermont, whose population hovers around five hundred.

When Jimmy's friend J. D. McClatchy asked me to speak at a memorial tribute to him at the New York Public Library, I told him it was a relief to find that unalterable plans made it impossible for me to be there on the appointed day. "In a way," I wrote, "Jimmy and I never knew each other as the people we grew up to become. What bound us together for fifty-five years was mostly the ancient days starting in 1940 when we loved

each other's mothers and grandmothers, and could laugh ourselves sick together over nothing in particular, and extravagantly admired each other's literary efforts, and had no idea
where we were going to go with our lives or how we were going
to get there, and spent little or no time thinking about it. It
would have been very hard for me to stand up and talk about
all that in the *Public* Library of all places, and almost equally
hard just to put into words how unhatched, unprotected, inno-
cent we were in those days and in some measure always became
again in each other's presence even when we were both pushing
seventy hard."

Looking back over the early years of our friendship, I am
drawn to the summer of 1948 as a turning point for both of us.
That June I had graduated from Princeton—one year late
because of an undistinguished hitch in the army—and had
lined up a job as assistant housemaster and teacher of English
at Lawrenceville, which Jimmy and I had both graduated from
in 1943. The job wasn't to begin until September, and to fill
up the intervening time and also to earn some money, I had
signed up to teach French at the summer session of the Hun
School in Princeton. I no longer remember just how the idea
first occurred to us, but at some point only a few weeks before
I was to show up at Hun, we decided that it would be much
more fun to spend the summer writing instead.

In my two post-army years at Princeton, I had come to
know William Meredith, whose first book of poems, *Love Letter
from an Impossible Land*, had come out a few years earlier and who
was an instructor in English at the time. In his rooms in Lower

Pine he used to give far and away the most enchanted cocktail parties I had ever attended or have ever attended since, where he served endless martinis in frosted silver glasses and where, in the spring, petals from a flowering plum sometimes drifted in through his mullioned windows to lie on the floor like snow. Colleagues from the English department like R. P. Blackmur, Donald Stauffer, and John Berryman came from time to time, together with occasional undergraduates like myself, and there were also friends he had made in the town of Princeton including a handful of beautiful young women, one of whom I fell fathomlessly in love with and on the starlit summer night of my twenty-first birthday on the balcony of the St. Regis roof in New York proposed matrimony to because—such was the world in those now almost unimaginable days—there seemed no other thinkable way to consummate our relationship. She wore her hair in two short pigtails, wore ballet slippers on her feet, could squirt through a gap in her teeth with remarkable accuracy, and at the same time had the good sense to turn me down. How things would have turned out for both of us if she had decided otherwise I shudder to imagine, but if we had had children they would now be past fifty, and that is shuddersome enough.

Another cocktail party regular was a man named Charles Shain, later the president of Connecticut College but at the time an English department colleague of Bill Meredith's, who with his New England wife, Jo, used to spend summers on Georgetown Island off the coast of Bath, Maine. Through the Shains Jimmy and I found a cottage to rent there, and at the zero hour I unconscionably wired the Hun School that for unspecified reasons I wouldn't be able to teach for them after all, and off we went, Jimmy to work on his *First Poems* and I on my first novel, *A Long Day's Dying*, which I had begun as a Princeton senior the year before. The New York publisher to whom I had sent the sixty pages I had written at college returned them with a note saying that not only did he find them completely unpublishable as they were, but he couldn't imagine anything I might do to change them or add to them that would make him feel differently. Why this didn't then and there destroy all my hopes of ever succeeding as a writer I no longer know, but for a wonder it didn't, and when the novel was finally published with considerable fanfare, he wrote me a second note asking if I could possibly forgive him for what he had said. I forgave him.

The Georgetown summer was a great success and in a way the last time Jimmy and I had with nothing to do but enjoy each other's company and take things as they came, before the world closed in on us and we went our separate ways to make something of ourselves as best we could with only the haziest notion in either of our cases as to what those somethings were to be. We wrote in the morning, Jimmy in one room and I in another, to the constant accompaniment of old 78-rpm records, which we took turns loading onto the portable phonograph—Stravinsky's *Petrouchka*, Mozart's violin and harpsichord sonatas adapted by Vronsky and Babin, if I have their names right after all these years, Satie's *Gymnopédies*, and the *Lieutenant Kije* suite of Prokofiev, to name only the few I remember. There were two broad, white-sanded beaches on the island's ocean side—Mile and Half Mile—which in those days, before they were turned into a state park and overrun with visitors, were almost always deserted, with no sign of human habitation except for a single weathered cottage in the dunes. They were separated by a tidal river that wound its way back into the salt marshes, and there, when the tide turned, we would enter it and with terns and gulls wheeling overhead would float on our backs through the reeds as far as its mouth, where deeply and not undangerously it flooded back into the sea. Jo Shain, a Hooker by birth and with Maine in her blood going back generations, used to give wonderful picnics there with the chill salt wind whipping us with sand as she heated canned Franco-American spaghetti with tomato sauce to the boiling point over a driftwood fire and then crumbled crisp bacon into it between her palms. Sometimes we dug for qua-hog clams to steam for supper when we got home, and Jo always warned us to be careful to come at them sideways with our hands cupped to avoid having our finger ends torn to pieces by their sharp shells.

Through the Shains we came to know many of the people who had been summering at Georgetown for years. There was the wiry little Russian Jewish sculptor, Morris Levine, who did the head of Jimmy on my windowsill, and his energetic, hos-pitable wife, Marge, who was built like a wrestler. Another sculptor, the famous Zorach, was also there, and I remember how once at a cocktail party at his house he produced the first tape recorder any of us had ever seen and, to demonstrate its extraordinary powers, recorded about half an hour's worth of utterly trivial chatter which he then insisted on playing back for us in full. There was Belle Lachaise, the widow of Gaston and sometime model for his great-busted nudes, with their swelling hips and monumental thighs tapering down like inverted pears to implausibly slender calves and tiny feet, although when we knew her she had long since turned into an elderly grande dame, addressed always as Madame Lachaise, who wore fringed shawls, a lace bandeau, and earrings down to her collarbone. There was also her sister-in-law, Elizabeth Nagle, who had been the longtime companion of Marsden Hartley in his Paris days and lived now in a one-room shack in the woods lashed to the trees to keep it from being blown away and when she came to parties always wore a pink silk slip because it was the fanciest thing she owned. She must have been in her eighties when we knew her, but, spry and game as a girl, she would go skinny-dipping with the rest of us off the Levines' dock after supper and once, when I unthinkingly lit up the night by striking a kitchen match to keep my pipe going, leaped into the Kennebec River like an old otter to preserve what was left of her modesty. Another time, during a game of Blind Man's Buff, she was cornered by a visiting Princeton friend of mine who, roaring like a bull with sweat pouring out from under his blindfold, tried to determine her gender as she cowered on top of the coffee table in her slip while Jimmy and I literally rolled on the floor in agonized mirth. Instead of a refrigerator we had only a wooden icebox, and we used to buy ice in large cakes from an enormous man named Gillie Lewis, with a puckered, beardless face and a piping voice, who wore rubbers on his stocking feet, had an old spaniel named Tyco, and was rumored to have been gelded by his mother as a child so she could be sure she would always have him around to take care of her in her old age.

We had electricity in our house but no plumbing—only a pump on the other side of the dirt road and a one-holer out in the barn from which you could watch an occasional porcupine laboriously clambering up a ladder to the loft above—and the only baths we had all summer were thanks to a pair of spinster schoolteachers who lived nearby. They raised angora rabbits for profit and told us that if we would help shear them, they could compensate us with a hot tub apiece. Most of the wool you could pull out easily and painlessly, but the "soiled mats," to use the ladies' term, had to be snipped away with scissors, and it was a delicate and unnerving business to do it without snipping through the fever-hot, tissue-paper-thin skin of their nether parts. "Soiled mats" became part of our vocabulary for many years afterwards, and for the rest of the summer we took care of our own either in the ocean with a cake of Lava soap or in a dishpan of water from the pump heated over the stove.

When the portable typewriter we shared for typing out our daily output broke down, we took it to a Neanderthal repairman in Bath who happened to be named Merrill, and when he tried to charge us a fee way beyond his original estimate, we sought advice from a local lawyer who told us that, possession being nine points of we knew what, the best thing we could do was somehow get it away from him when he wasn't looking and then send him a check for the amount originally agreed upon. While one of us engaged him in conversation, the other somehow managed to get hold of the typewriter and hotfoot it out the door, but how we managed so perilous a maneuver without getting our skulls bashed in, and what that other Merrill did when he saw what had happened, I can no longer remember, and the only other one who could tell me is no longer around to do so.

If it hadn't been for that summer in Maine, would I have found some other time, some other place, to write that first novel? Would Jimmy have written those first poems, which Knopf published in 1951, a year after publishing me? One way or another I suspect the answer is yes, but would they have been the same novel, the same poems? I suspect not. And I suspect too that no other circumstances we might have contrived separately would have come even close to matching those easy, companionable, nurturing, celibate, insulated days ringing with laughter that we spent together before our different worlds began to harden around us and we became in many ways two different people.

A Different Person is the title Jimmy gave to his memoirs of the year 1950 when, so soon after Georgetown, he set sail for Europe, putting everything behind him—his old life, his old friends, his tycoon father, who in the end proved surprisingly better able to understand and accept his son's differentness than his bright and charming Southern mother, who was as totally devoted to him, her only child, as she was totally devastated by what, like his father, she too had discovered by then to be his homosexuality. It was his whole world that Jimmy put behind him when he left, including the kind of poems he had fashioned out of it, which in the memoir he describes as "verbal artifacts, metered and rhymed to be sure, shaped and polished and begemmed, but set on the page with no thought of their being uttered by a living voice." Many of them were the poems that he worked on so diligently with Stravinsky and Mozart dithering away in the background, while across the downstairs hall I labored over my novel about a fat man named Tristram Bone, his pet monkey, and his urbane, leisured little circle of friends with their tragi-comic inability to communicate with each other what it was like to be who they truly and secretly were. For good luck I asked Jimmy to write a single sentence that I could insert somewhere in the book, and the one he came up with, duplicating my preposterously mandarin style at the time, was as follows: "But then as not sufficiently punished by his slow, melancholy presence for the ugliness of her words, she saw and managed somehow to recognize, who else was witness to her humiliation, Maroo, advancing from the groin of the hall as she had never, for Elizabeth, advanced before." Looking back, I think I see now how Jimmy and I were not much better than my characters at communicating with each other the innermost truth of who we were, not, I think, because it was a truth that either of us shied away from sharing—what made us such fast friends was that there was no topic we shied away from—but because we were only beginning to glimpse it ourselves. The selves we were beginning to grow into that summer were still in the shadowy wings awaiting their entrance cues—the minister who wrote books and the poet who, when I asked him once if in his commerce with the various deities of the Ouija board poems he had ever found any he felt like worshiping, said, "Oh, I *adore* God!" in exactly the same way he would have said he adored Ethel Merman. In the meantime we went on being the only selves we knew how to be just then—picnicking on those beautiful, vacant beaches, shopping in Bath, taking turns reading *The Wings of the Dove* out loud to each other on evenings when there was nothing else going on, and such like. Often, when visitors came, one of us by prearrangement would ask the other to read out loud something from his own work in hopes that they would find it as wonderful as we invariably did ourselves. We still had a long way to go before finding our grown-up selves and true voices.

As he had hoped, Jimmy came back from his *Wanderjahr* well on his way at least to becoming a different person, and in his memoirs he describes the process with an astonishing richness of detail. He remembers the operas he heard and who sang what, together with paintings he saw and the friends he saw them with. He remembers restaurants he went to and even particular meals he ate at them. He remembers all the places he stayed including the Hotel Maricel in Mallorca where I visited him and a friend of his for a few weeks in December of 1950 because it had turned so cold in England, where I was working on my second novel, that the only way I could keep warm was by getting into bed and trying to write there, only to find that more often than not I fell asleep instead. Again and again he even remembers conversations verbatim, and where they took place and who said what and to whom.

Because he wanted to know if I thought various of his friends and particularly his mother would be hurt or offended by what he had written so candidly about them, he asked me to read the typescript before he sent it off to the publisher, and with something less than full conviction I told him that, although his portraits were by no means always flattering, I thought that in the long run their subjects would be able to live with them—not hung over the living-room mantel maybe, but in the upstairs hall at least, or a little-used bedroom. Much of the story he tells was familiar to me because I had been in on at least the fringes of it. I knew about his psychoanalysis, although Dr. Detre himself I think I never met. I knew and loved his mother and had met his father a number of times, a short, soft-spoken, self-possessed man whose face was covered—as Jimmy's became in time—with tiny wrinkles, like a piece of paper smoothed out after having been wadded up for a long time in a tight ball. There was nothing especially striking about either his appearance or his manner, and yet he had only to enter the room for you to feel the power of his presence. I also knew or at least had met most of Jimmy's friends of those days and through his marvelous long letters had kept in touch with his comings and goings.

But what I had not known and was totally unprepared for were the sexual adventures that he recounts in detail—the one-night stands, the furtive assignations in Roman latrines, the affairs within affairs, the sheer abundance of lovers. It was not so much that I was shocked by it—in my virginal fantasies, I had been just as promiscuous and insatiable—but that I was appalled by what struck me as the loneliness and sadness and seediness of it all. It was hard to believe that there was so much about my old friend that he had never told me, or, if in some way he had by implication half told it, that I had never heard because I didn't choose to hear it. I found myself depressed for days by the book and could only believe that he would do himself irreparable harm by writing it all down with such unrelenting honesty for the world to read. I didn't see how anybody could help thinking the worse of him because of it. And I suppose part of my depression was the realization of how meager and inhibited my own sexual experience had been by comparison. If I had missed out on the sadness and seediness, I had missed out also, through timidity and squeamishness, on much that being young and alive and both in love with and part of the world's beauty is all about.

At the end of each chapter of *A Different Person*, there is an italicized postscript in which Jimmy looks at the story he is telling about the past from the perspective of the present, and in one of these he sets down a conversation with his mother that in actuality never took place. "Don't imagine, son, that these are things people need to know," he has her say, and then there is a paragraph in which he tries to explain to her why he found it necessary and important to say them anyway. The explanation struck me as so dim and hard to follow, and at the same time so crucial to an understanding not just of the book but of Jimmy himself, that I wrote him suggesting that he give it another try. His answer was, "I've been cudgeling my wits to clarify, perhaps expand, that passage you found cryptic. At present it seems that to open it up would set off such a flood as to afflict my readers with hydrophobia. But we'll see. I love challenges!" I have never checked back on the typescript to see if he made any changes at all, but even if he did, they didn't seem to help much. "Over the years, the forbidden fruit of self-disclosure grew ever more tempting" is one of the things he says, and having disclosed in print a good many secrets of my own, I can understand what he meant by the tempting impulse to do so, to give the past at least a semblance of order and keep the record more or less straight. I know also that it takes a certain kind of courage to do it, of self-confidence anyway, and that if you do it right, you are rewarded by a sense of having laid down a burden and let fresh air into a room too long kept shuttered. But still I wish that he hadn't done it. And there was little about him afterwards that gave me the sense that the doing of it had added much to his peace.

His affairs were legion, but reading the book I had the feeling that there had been little love in them, little even of very satisfactory friendship in them, and I ended up believing that, although his experience had been vastly wider and more varied than mine in ways other than just sexually, he nonetheless had missed out on much that it seems to me at its fullest and richest life has to offer. Reading his pages was like listening to music with the treble turned way up and the bass turned so nearly off altogether that the deeper resonances are almost entirely absent. Elizabeth Bishop, one of Jimmy's many poet friends, said somewhere that one reason she chose to live in South America was that it kept her in touch with what she called "old-fashioned life," and that was just what for years I had felt, as the memoirs seemed to confirm, Jimmy had more or less lost touch with. The kinds of things that make people weep, either for sadness or for joy, were things that with his extraordinary gift for wit and irony he managed more often than not to deflect or to transform almost beyond recognition. The only real tears I could imagine him weeping were poetic tears.

I suppose that as a child he had had enough of old-fashioned life to last him permanently, starting with his parents' messy divorce when he was eleven and the resulting estrangement from his father, soon to be followed by his being sent off to Lawrenceville, where, as he describes it in a touching autobiographical poem called "Days of 1941 and '44," he was much of the time tormented and ridiculed by the other boys. Fat, effeminate, bespectacled, with braces on his teeth, and nicknamed Toots, he was easy game, and the only weapon he had for defending himself was that same wit, that same irony, that for the rest of his life he used for fending off the worst and to some extent, I can't help believing, also the best. Much of what I think kept the two of us dearest friends for all those years, which in so many ways divided us, was that there always remained between us a measure of unquestioning trust and unending sympathy that from time to time enabled him to risk being as unarmed and defenseless with me as he was with Dr. Detre. Maybe that is why, along with his mother, his psychiatrist and I were the two people he phoned from the hospital to say good-bye to on the last full day he lived before letting down his defenses for good.

The "Uglies" was what we started calling each other way back in our early days of knowing each other—a term I first came across in E. Nesbit's masterpiece, *The Enchanted Castle*, where they are the grotesque mannequins made of bolsters, hockey sticks, gloves stuffed with handkerchiefs, and paper masks for faces, whom the children bring to life and then spend chapters trying to escape. Uglies, as we conceived them, were people who much of the time felt beleaguered and out of step, who didn't usually laugh or cry at the same kinds of things that other people did, and who both rejoiced in not being like everybody else and also of course longed to be. An Ugly was bookish, introspective, completely nonathletic and tended to feel awkward and helpless and lost, especially on occasions when the rest of the world seemed to be having the time of their lives. We decided that as far as we knew, there were only two Uglies in existence, and we were they. We also decided that in case the nuclear holocaust should ever come about and we were left alive, we would meet at some natural landmark large enough to ensure its escape from destruction. The Grand Canyon was the one we hit on for some reason and then realized that neither of us had any clear idea where the Grand Canyon was. We realized too that there was no end to the things that Uglies had no clear idea of, but at least they had each other, and for all the decades of our friendship, we kept on occasionally signing the letters that went back and forth between us "the Other One" to remind us.

On my sixty-fifth birthday, Jimmy sent me a miniature pair
of antique dice and a quatrain to go with them:

Exactly sixty-five
Times by now time has thrown
His rattling dice of bone
And guess who's still alive!
　　the UGLIES!

I managed to fit both poem and dice into a small plastic
shadowbox that sits on the windowsill not far from Jimmy's
bronze head from Georgetown days. It is a good, if idealized,
likeness, and for years Hellen, his mother, had it with her in
Atlanta until the two of them for some reason or other decided
that they would turn it over to me. The transfer took place at
the apartment in Palm Beach where Hellen spent winters. My
wife and I had a drink with them one afternoon and then,
amidst a good deal of comic groaning at the weight of the
thing, lugged it down in the elevator and with Jimmy's help
loaded it into the trunk of the car.

For years it spent winters outside on our terrace in Florida,
its cheeks often wet with rain or its hair displaying the chalky
memento of some passing bird. The rest of the year, when we
went north, it stayed locked up in the dark of the bar closet
with only a bronze dragonfly and a lot of glasses for company.
It was not until after Jimmy was swallowed up by the dark
himself that I decided to bring it back with us to Vermont.

Placing it on the windowsill facing straight forward made it look too much like a votive shrine, so I turned it enough to the left to give it a view of Buddha's slender hand on the mantel. Jimmy, age twenty-two, is looking slightly upward with his lips parted. Something seems to have startled him. Maybe it is nothing more than finding himself in that green-carpeted, book-lined room full of stillness with usually no one but his oldest friend for company.

three

As you enter the Magic Kingdom, biographies are immediately to your right in floor-to-ceiling shelves, hundreds of them ranging all the way from James Agee, Thomas Aquinas, and Louis Armstrong, who crowd each other way up in the left-hand corner, down to Oscar Wilde, the Duke of Windsor, Virginia Woolf, Wordsworth, and, last of all, Captain R. F. Zogbaum, whose privately printed memoirs, like a great many other books I own, I have never read. ("Why on earth would I want to do that?" a friend of mine answered when somebody asked him once if he had read all his.) Captain Zogbaum is there—onetime commandant of the Naval Air Station at Pensacola and commander of the aircraft carrier *Saratoga*—because I used to see him as a boy when he had retired to Tryon, North Carolina, where we were then living, and because my cousin Tony Wick married his son Rufus. The son of an artist praised by Rudyard Kipling, he was a striking-looking old man with thin sandy hair and part of one ear missing who, when ladies he admired came for tea, would always pipe them into his house with a bosun's whistle. When I think of him, I can all but see him entering the room with a stiff little limp but straight as a mast—the patrician profile, the clipped, faintly British way of speaking, the heathery tweed jacket worn threadbare at the elbows.

Others enter with him—Satchmo, his lips wobbling around his ecstatic, bojangles smile, G. K. Chesterton, colossal in cape and pince-nez, tiny little Gerard Manley Hopkins. Mozart peers mouselike out of an oversized wig. Franklin Roosevelt rolls through the door in his chair. Clara Barton is there—Naya's mother, who died a year after having her, was her cousin—to say nothing of Lewis Carroll, Mahatma Gandhi, and Dr. John Donne. Scores of others are close behind them, but the room is not big enough for them all, thank heaven, and they vanish so that only the biographies are left. Thank heaven too that the biographies are silent, as are all the other books as well—fiction, poetry, drama, religion, and what-have-you.

Shakespeare is not saying anything, and neither is L. Frank Baum. The Duc de Saint-Simon, the Buddha, Dostoyevski, and Paul Tillich are all holding their tongues. Not a peep out of Abraham Lincoln, Meister Eckhart, or Emily Dickinson. Even Walt Whitman and the prophet Jeremiah are for the moment speechless. The air of the Magic Kingdom is electric with the silence they are keeping. What would I have been if I had never heard them break it? What would I have failed to see if they had not pointed it out to me, and what would I have never heard without their ears to hear it through? What would I have missed loving without them to show me its loveliness? What marvelous jokes would have been lost on me? What tears would I have never found the heart to shed? And yet no less a gift is the mercy now of their keeping still with the sunlight lying in squares on the green carpet and the whole room holding its breath. They are there for when I need them, but in the meanwhile there is not a word out of any of them. Like wise parents, they are giving me room to be myself. They are giving me this room.

My real parents and grandparents and assorted forebears are to be found in the small shelf-lined room that is the entryway to the Magic Kingdom. On the left it opens into the library, and straight ahead is the hallway to the office where I type on the computer what I have written out in pen and ink. In the shelves on one wall of the room you enter by are extra copies of the thirty-odd books I have written since the first one in 1950, together with my collection of CDs and tapes and the equipment for playing them. On another wall are old LPs, some of them dating back as far as the late '40s, with shirt cardboards for dividers to mark such categories as Choral, Baroque, 19th Century, Jazz, Musical Comedy, Personalities including Beatrice Lillie, Jimmy Durante, Mae West, Hal Holbrook as Mark Twain, and so on. It is the third wall where the family archives are. On the bottom shelves are a number of grey cardboard boxes each marked with one family surname or another. They contain dozens of old photographs, daguerreotypes, letters, genealogies, and such documents as my grandfather Kuhn's

1887 diploma from National Normal University in Lebanon, Ohio, and my Buechner grandparents' marriage certificate. Knowing of my interest in such things, relatives have been passing them on to me for years.

In one of these boxes is the penciled manuscript of my first literary effort, a cliffhanger entitled *The Voyage of Mr. and Mrs. Cloth*, which I wrote in Washington, D.C., where we lived in 1932 because, through a Princeton roommate, my father had a minor job in the circulation department of the *Evening Star* there. As Dr. Freud would be quick to note, Mrs. Cloth, the mother, is a powerhouse who successfully fends off an attack by cannibals, whereas Mr. Cloth, the father, is a shadowy figure of whom I say little except that he was "fiddling with the machinery" as he tried to effect their getaway in a motorboat. I remember still the roundabout way I arrived at the name Cloth. A real name like Smith or Brown, I reasoned, would sound too much like a name I made up just to *sound* real, whereas if I used a name that sounded as obviously made up as Cloth, people would think it must be real because otherwise I would never have used it. I will leave it again to Dr. Freud to decide whether another reason for using it was that in some subterranean part of myself I sensed at the age of six that cloth was about as inadequate a defense as any you could find against not only cannibal attacks, but such other hostile forces as the Depression, my father's inability to hold a job for long, his problem with alcohol, and my mother's scathing denunciations of him which I was constantly terrified would blow the only world I knew sky high.

On the shelf above the grey boxes are a number of miscellaneous volumes, one of which is my father's baby book. It was put out by Brentano's in 1891 with pages of heavy stock and drawings by Frances Brundage to illustrate Baby's First Steps, Baby's First Words, Baby's First Outing, and so on, all of them filled out in my grandmother's hand. Of his first words, as she set them down, two were German ("Ei" and "nein") and the third "baby." For his first outing, when he was less than a month old, she wrote, "He was placed in a washbasket on the top piazza of our country home overlooking the bay and the ocean and all of Manhattan Beach," which was the gingerbread house on Millionaires' Row in Sheepshead Bay that belonged to her father, old Herman Balthasar Scharmann. His First Laugh took place on December 7, 1898, but she does not say what occasioned it.

On the page for Baby's Health Record she describes how at the age of six he underwent a minor operation on the muscle of his left eye that left him with a slightly drooping eyelid and a tendency for the rest of his life to hold his head a little to one side. My mother used to make fun of him for this, and as shameful a memory as any I have is of a time when as a child I was sitting beside her in the back seat of the car with him at the wheel, and I said, *"Regardez la tête"* loud enough for him to hear. I suppose that as her idolater and helpless thrall I was trying to curry favor with her by both joining her in her mockery and deepening it by using French, as she did when she didn't want my brother and me to understand what she was saying. As far as I remember, my father just sat there in silence, and that is how it always was. I can't remember a single instance of his defending himself against even her bitterest and most derisive attacks, let alone ever taking the offensive. Poor Mr. Cloth. If only he had turned around and knocked our heads together, it might have saved the day for him, might have saved not only his soul, but hers. And maybe mine as well.

Into the baby book I have slipped an affidavit sent to my mother soon after his death in 1936—he left no will—stating that his entire estate consisted of a Chevrolet sedan valued at two hundred dollars, the same one on whose running board he sat with his head in his hands as the acrid blue fumes filled the garage of our house on Hawthorne Road in Essex Fells, New Jersey. On one of the rare occasions when I risked speaking out loud to my mother about this terrible thing that had happened, I remember asking her why we hadn't gotten another car to replace it, and she said it was because we couldn't afford to.

A Xerox I made of the blank page at the end of *Gone with the Wind* where my father penciled his note to her is in the baby book too—Baby's Last Words—and so is a letter my cousin and almost exact contemporary Tom Buechner wrote me many years later describing his memory of the morning his family got the news. His father, my uncle Tom, was my father's youngest brother, and when he heard it, he cried, which my cousin had never seen him do before. "My mother told me Uncle Fred was dead and to stay in my room," my cousin wrote. "Later, I went out and there on the front steps he sat with his shoulders going up and down but no sound coming out. I couldn't bear it, it was as if he had left me forever. I ran away as fast as I could back up away from our house on streets I had never seen before. When I got tired, I walked away and away. After a long time—it seemed a long time—someone in a car stopped. I guess they knew me; they took me home."

It was some eight years later that as a Princeton undergraduate attending a prom at the Rosemary School I got a message from the headmistress's office to call Mr. Tom Buechner. Because Uncle Tom had recently baled me out of some college debts, he was the one I thought was meant, and I asked for him when somebody answered the phone. There was an awkward silence, and then my cousin Tom came on. That morning, he said, his father had returned from getting the Sunday papers, discussed breakfast with the maid, and then went upstairs to his bathroom and shot himself.

Above the grey boxes there is a shelf of photograph albums, the kind they used to make that are about four times longer from front to back than they are high with black cloth or leatherette covers and black pages held together at the spine with grommets and black cord. Many of the pages have come loose, and some have become so brittle that they tend to break off around the edges when you're handling them. Some of the leatherette bindings have also begun to go soft and crumbly. If the photographs are identified, it has been done in white ink.

One of the albums was my mother's as a young unmarried woman and is devoted entirely to holidays she spent in Lake Placid—along with her parents, her younger sister, Ruth, and her brother, Jimmy, the youngest of the three—toward the end of, and for a few years after, the First World War. With the possible exception of Bermuda, where we went to live a few months after my father's death, there was no part of her life that she so much enjoyed reminiscing about. The pictures are all black and white, needless to say, and most of them taken at the Lake Placid Club, where everybody stayed in those days and everybody knew everybody else. You see them, old and young together, in their enormous fur coats like characters out of *The Gold Rush*, in their galoshes, calf-high leather boots, knickerbockers, checked lumberjack shirts. The ladies of Naya's generation wear skirts to their ankles and have their hands tucked in muffs. My mother and Aunt Ruth, barely in their twenties, are stunning in jodhpurs with scarves dangling to their knees and hats with their broad brims turned up in front like a pair of village idiots, my mother said. These were her flapper days, when there were more than enough beaux to go around what with the army training camp at Plattsburgh nearby, which my father attended the summer of 1916, when he was eighteen and my mother twenty, and where they possibly met for the first time. Because my grandfather's coal business was booming, home was in a posh residential area in a suburb of Pittsburgh called East Liberty, where they lived in a big, rich man's house on Woodland Road with the likes of Andy Mellon and the Fricks for neighbors, and one evening at a dance Dick Mellon asked her to marry him, which she didn't do, she told me, because she didn't think he really loved her and because she didn't think she really loved him either.

Most of the Lake Placid photographs were taken in winter with everybody on snowshoes or skijoring behind horses or tobogganing or watching figure-skating exhibitions or ice hockey, but there are a good many summer ones too, one of which shows a number of nattily dressed people at a sporting event of some kind, maybe tennis, the women all wearing elegant hats and long skirts and the men in jackets and ties. The older people are sitting on folding chairs and the younger on the sunny grass in front of them. In the foreground of the photograph is my father in white flannels and a dark blazer with a bow tie and saddle shoes. He is loosely clasping his knees with his arms and looking off to the left, a faint smile on his lips, his face in profile. Next to him is my mother in a straw hat with a large, downward-turning brim and a dark jersey over a blouse that has a wide white collar and cuffs. Next to her is her fifteen-year-old brother, Jimmy, in knickerbockers. It was a historic occasion, I seem to remember my mother once telling me, because on the very next day, July 17, 1922, she and my father ran off to be married at Trinity Episcopal Church in nearby Plattsburgh with only Uncle Jimmy and a Pittsburgh friend named Joe Young to sign their names as witnesses in the little wedding service booklet I still have in one of the grey boxes. They drove on then to the Chateau Frontenac in Quebec for their wedding night.

The reason they had to elope was that my grandfather Kuhn was violently opposed to the match. Bald as an egg except for a fringe of grey hair, he had a shaggy moustache and mild blue eyes and always let Naya do most of the talking because he so admired how well she did it and because he was by nature on the retiring side. But when it came to the subject of any of his children getting married, he turned into a raging maniac. According to my mother, the only reason he didn't put up a terrible fuss about Aunt Ruth was that the man she chose was from a distinguished Youngstown family named Wick, but although I was only a small boy at the time, I can still remember how, when Uncle Jimmy's engagement was announced in the New York papers, there was such an explosion that we all ran for cover. The engagement was called off, and Uncle Jimmy remained a bachelor for the rest of his days.

My mother, I think, was her father's favorite—the firstborn as well as the family beauty—but in spite of that, or because of it, she was also the one he seems always to have come down on hardest and according to her used to spank unmercifully as a child. If anybody had explained to him about covert incest, he would have died of horror, but with the possible exception of Dick Mellon, he violently objected to any man who ever threatened to take her away from him, and when my father turned up, what he apparently found most objectionable about him was, ironically, his German name. As far as he was concerned, his own name, Kuhn, was Pennsylvania *Dutch* and as such put him in a different category altogether. What was more, there had been Kuhns around since the eighteenth century when one of them—named Adam like my grandfather's father—was the first president of the Royal College of Physicians and Surgeons in prerevolutionary Philadelphia, whereas the Buechners didn't arrive until after 1848. In any case, for the first few years following his daughter's elopement, he apparently didn't so much as allow her name to be mentioned in his presence. The story is that he had all her pictures taken down in the Woodland Road house, and Naya was able to see her only on surreptitious visits to New York, which was where she and my father lived in the early years of their marriage—at 14 East 96th Street, the apartment I was brought home to as a newborn infant just a few days before their fourth wedding anniversary. Why have I remembered that address all these years when at the time I was too young to remember anything?

"Romantic" and "glamorous" were among the words my mother used for describing the Lake Placid days. Everybody was so young then, she said. The world was so young. She said nobody ever had such wonderful times again as they had back then when there was all the money in the world and nobody seemed to have anything to worry about. "Divine" was another of her words. The divine times they had falling in and out of love, the sleigh rides by moonlight, the parties, the divine-looking young men. "In my wildest dreams as a girl I never believed it would come to this" was one of the classic ways her excoriations of my father began, which was to say that in her wildest dreams at Lake Placid she never for a moment believed she would end up married to a man who could barely afford a single maid-of-all-work to take care of them, never believed she would end up in New *Jersey* of all places. But there, sitting on the grass in her broad-brimmed straw hat on that summer day in 1922, she had no wilder dreams than those whose hero was that same man, sitting beside her in his bow tie and blazer with his arms around his knees.

He was twenty-four years old at the time—she was twenty-six—and had been captain of the water-polo team at Princeton and danced divinely and looked a little like Rudolph Valentino with his olive complexion and strong young swimmer's body. Searching for some clue to the terrible things that happened to their marriage, I asked a woman who had known them back then what they had been like. I thought she might be able to tell me something she had glimpsed in them, some fatal foreshadowing. They were married for fourteen years, and there is not a single photograph of my father taken toward the last few of them that shows him smiling. His handsome face has gone hollow-cheeked and skull-like. His deep-set eyes are lost in shadow.

Without a moment's hesitation the woman I had questioned said simply, "I wanted to be just like them." And who wouldn't have?

Like the books in the library, the old photographs and the old letters are silent. They too are leaving me room to be myself. They are letting me be, as most of the time I try also to let them be, passing by the grey boxes as I enter the Magic Kingdom without a sideward glance. I do not want to stir them up or be stirred up by them. But even in their silence they are always present. My father has been dead for more than sixty years, but I doubt that a week has gone by without my thinking of him. In recent years I doubt that a single day has gone by. Who on earth was he? Who on earth would he have lived to become? He could even conceivably still be alive to see his hundredth birthday this summer, just as Jimmy Merrill's mother, born the same month of the same year, will see hers. Who on earth would I have become if he had lived long enough to get me through my growing up? What would he have to say to me now, or I to him?

At least I know what I would say to him as he sits there on the grass next to my mother with his face turned to look at something that nobody else seems to be noticing. Shadowed by her hat brim, my mother's gaze appears to be directed toward the photographer, but it is not the photographer she is seeing. She is seeing beyond him to what she knows is going to happen the next day. Her eyes are filled with her secret, and her expression is very grave. Who knows all that she is seeing?

I would say to my father, "Don't do it. Get out of it any way you can, for both your sakes. You would never dream where the path you have chosen is going to lead you. Make a break for it while there's still time."

But why should he listen? There isn't a man at Lake Placid who isn't in love with the girl at his side. The rector of Trinity Church will be waiting for them the next day. The room at the Chateau Frontenac has been booked. It will all happen as planned, and among other things that will happen, I will happen. So how can I wish undone this thing they are on the threshold of doing without wishing myself undone? Even though it will cost my father his life at the age of thirty-eight, and even though it will mean my mother's taking to her grave just short of her ninety-second birthday a burden of guilt and regret and self-condemnation that as far as I know she never spoke about to a living soul let alone to me, I would not have missed the shot at the world that their misalliance gave me. Can I make it up to them somehow—by treasuring away their youth and beauty in the grey boxes and telling about it, by honoring them as best I can for having been father and mother to me as best they could, by forgiving them and asking their forgiveness? Behind them, in folding chairs, sit two middle-aged women with an elderly woman between them. They are obviously a threesome and are wearing large hats one of which has an ostrich feather overlapping the brim in back. They are the three Fates, of course, and Atropos is the one with the ostrich feather. Her right hand is concealed behind my father's shoulders and in it the fatal shears.

If I have words to speak to these relics I keep, they also have words to speak to me. One relic is the *Mark Twain* scrapbook that my grandmother Buechner kept up virtually all her adult life and referred to always as "the family annals." Invented by Mark Twain himself and bound in stamped brown buckram, it is a large, chunky volume, by now more or less falling to pieces, with a hundred and fifty numbered pages each with three columns of gummed lines on it which, when moistened, hold the scraps in place. The first sixty-three pages have to do mainly with my grandmother's father, Herman Balthasar Scharmann, who was a leading figure in the German-American community of Brooklyn in his time. He was born in Giessen, Germany, not far from Frankfurt, in 1838 and brought to this country by his parents when he was five years old.

There are numerous articles in German from the *Freie Presse* about his various business dealings as head of Scharmann and Sons, a brewery, and such of his many civic activities as helping to swing the German-American vote to Grover Cleveland in the election of 1884. There are assorted mementos of his days as president of the New York Liederkrantz, his singing society, the United States Brewers Association, and the Kegel Klub, where he bowled regularly on Fridays. He was also a director of the Manufacturers Trust along with various other financial institutions as well as a member of the Brooklyn Board of Education. There is an article about the trip around the world that he took after his wife's death with two of their five daughters, and several columns about his memories of the California Gold Rush when, as a child of twelve, he accompanied his father and a company of Germans across the continent in a covered wagon with both his mother and a baby sister dying along the way. When he himself died in 1920, all the major papers carried his obituary. "Herman B. Scharmann, 82, Pioneer Brewer, 'Forty-Niner,' dies. One of Only Eight of Party of 72 to Reach California Alive. Banker and Clubman," is the headline of the one in the *Brooklyn Eagle*, and a later piece reports that his estate was valued at $470,292, which together with a good deal of valuable Brooklyn real estate was left to his daughters and one surviving son, more than enough at that time to keep them in ease for the rest of their days.

Although I was born six years too late to know him myself, I remember how for the rest of his daughters' long lives, his maxims were still on their lips, like "Never put anything off because of the weather" (as I wrote in an earlier account of him, it is easier to imagine the weather's putting something off because of him) and "Never put on your bathing suit without going in the water"; and I remember too how, even when they had become old ladies, at the mere mention of his name their eyes were apt to fill with tears. It was not until she was in her eighties that one of them, my great-aunt Emma Zinsser, started talking about his shadow side—how he ruled his family the way Kaiser Wilhelm ruled the Fatherland, the way he treated his gentle-spirited wife whom he met when he played the part of her father in some amateur theatricals, his tyrannical rages—but in the Mark Twain scrapbook, he is the unblemished hero.

Then suddenly, on page sixty-four, I am among people I know. There is a newspaper announcement of my mother's engagement which names my grandfather along with Naya as doing the announcing, although I am sure he had fits if anybody dared show it to him. Accompanying the announcement of the marriage there is also a newspaper photo of my mother that makes her look like a silent-movie star. It is placed next to another one of her from a year or so later in a toque and long string of beads at some charity bazaar in Greenwich, Connecticut, where she and my father lived as newlyweds in a stone cottage belonging to the painter John Twachtman. With an arch caption saying that on a hike in the Adirondacks she stopped to feed a hungry grey squirrel, there is another obviously posed photograph from the rotogravure section of the *New York Tribune* of January 1924 that shows her fallen face forward in the snow at Lake Placid with her snowshoes flopping in the air over her, and just above it my grandmother has pasted the announcement of my brother Jamie's birth four years later. Although chronologically speaking it should be considerably farther ahead in the book, my father's three-line obituary is also on this page: "Buechner, C. Fred jr, suddenly, at his home, Essex Fells, New Jersey, on Nov. 21, 1936. Funeral Private." Suddenly. There was no funeral. My grandmother had to turn back through many pages to find what she considered the right place for it underneath the picture of my mother in her toque and not far from a notice of my having won first prize in an intercollegiate poetry contest at Mount Holyoke when I was a senior at Princeton.

The rest of the book is a rich compendium of family lore, the births, marriages, deaths, and assorted comings and goings of innumerable relatives as they found their way by one route or another into the public press. The two daughters of my grandmother's sister Emma Zinsser made good marriages—one to Lewis Douglas, Roosevelt's Budget Director and later ambassador to England, and the other to John McCloy, U.S. High Commissioner of Germany after the Second World War and head of the World Bank—and there are many articles about them and their families. My grandfather Buechner's obituary is there. It is as tiny as my father's, his oldest son and namesake, who had died just five days earlier. Some pages later, Uncle Tom's is there too, dated April 22, 1944, placed directly underneath an article from the *Herald Tribune* announcing some promotion he had been given at the Ted Bates agency the fall before. In the accompanying picture, he looks trim and successful.

As each death came along, my grandmother must have snipped the notice of it out of the paper within a day or two of its happening or even on the day itself, then searched back for the right page, moistened a gummed strip or two, and stuck it in place. Her tears as a rule came quickly and easily, but I do not picture her shedding any as she performed this necrological task. I picture her instead stumping effortfully into the dining room and ringing for Rosa the maid to bring her the family annals there so she could work on them at the carved oak table with its lion-headed chairs. Like her father before her, she was a survivor. Like him, she put nothing off because of the weather. I often saw her weep briefly for him years after his death, and about small things that upset her or for some reason touched her. But when it came to the devastating things, I cannot see her crying, maybe because she was too busy surviving. I know at least that the one time the subject of the devastating things ever came up between her and me, she remained dry-eyed.

It took place in her living room in New York one late afternoon when she was eighty or so. She was sitting, as she always did, in her chair by the window with her little radio on the sill at her left and her sewing stand at her right. The fringed Tiffany lamp standing behind her was not lit, and the room was filled with dusk. Maybe it was because we could see each other only dimly that the few words we managed to speak became for the first and only time possible between us. I remember them only as quiet, shapeless words. I'm not sure I even mentioned my father by name, and I don't think she did either, either his or Uncle Tom's or my grandfather's. I have no memory of what we said to each other or any sense that questions were answered or ghosts laid to rest. I remember only that together we looked for a few minutes into the saddest, darkest place we either of us knew. For once both our guards were down and the difference between our generations meant nothing, and it was the closest we had ever been or would ever be again.

Nobody seemed to know or care much about what happened to the Mark Twain scrapbook after my grandmother's death in 1958. Her only daughter, Betty, the youngest of her four children, eventually settled with her husband only a few miles from us in Vermont, and from time to time I would ask her if she had any idea what had become of it, but she never seemed altogether sure what I was talking about, and in time I decided that it must have simply gotten lost in the shuffle somehow when my grandmother's apartment was dismantled, possibly even thrown out with a lot of old letters and other things that nobody seemed to think worth saving. In any case, when Aunt Betty finally died years later, her husband phoned me one day to say that while sorting through her belongings he'd come across a few he thought I might be interested in and invited me to come over and take a look at them. He had them laid out on a bridge table when I got there, and even though I hadn't seen it for twenty years or more, and from the other side of the room at that, I immediately spotted what I had hoped for so long to find, its back cover loose and the front one almost off its hinges altogether. The discovery brought with it two voices from the grave.

The first voice was my aunt's. She must have known all along exactly what I was after and exactly where it was, but was simply damned if she wanted me to have it. Her reason I was quick to guess, because in a way I suppose I had always known it. For all the years that we lived within a stone's throw of each other, we seldom saw each other, and I'm willing to believe that the fault was mostly mine. During my childhood, my grandmother, who was our sole means of support, would come from time to time to read the riot act to my mother, telling her that she was living too extravagantly, not facing up to her responsibilities, making mama's boys out of her two sons, or whatever else she felt needed saying; and either because I witnessed some of these occasions myself, or because my mother described them so vividly, I picture Aunt Betty in the background grimly seconding everything her mother said. In other words from as far back as I can remember, my aunt was an intimidating figure and for as long as she lived the only person, I think, of whom I was genuinely afraid, with her deep, gravelly voice from years of heavy smoking, her mannish looks, and more even than my grandmother her unsettling habit of fixing you with her eye and saying exactly what was on her mind. She told me once that I had made a bad mistake in giving up my teaching job at Exeter to be a full-time writer—writing books was something I should have done, if at all, she said, only after retirement—and the belligerence with which she uttered such judgments always made me quail, so that even in my fifties I felt tongue-tied and defenseless in her presence.

My other reason for steering clear of her was that she knew so much that she wouldn't tell me about the dark mystery of the family she had grown up in, which had produced three alcoholics and two suicides. What in God's name had gone wrong? What sort of parents had my grandparents been or failed to be? What had my grandfather been like, who was always a shadowy figure as I remember him, sitting off at the edge of things not saying much as he nursed his perpetual high-ball? And what especially could she tell me about my father, who I knew was the one of her three brothers whom she had especially adored? But if ever the conversation showed signs of heading that way, she would change it in no time flat, and the one time I dared bring up the two suicides specifically and asked her what she thought was behind them, she snapped back that they had had nothing whatever to do with each other. My father's was because he had lost all his money through the bad investments that my other grandfather had gotten him into, and Uncle Tom's was because his bad eyes had kept him out of the armed services during the Second World War, and that was that. She wouldn't touch any of it with a ten-foot pole, I sup-pose because not all her courage and strength were up to facing whatever it was that she must have known in her heart, and I'm sure she deeply resented my probing. For all I know, maybe she was as afraid of me as I was of her.

At the same time, however, she must have loved me in a way, as in a way I also loved her. She had had literary aspirations as a young woman and admired me for such success as I'd had as a writer. I was also the son of her favorite brother, after all, and in an old album of hers that I was given along with the Mark Twain scrapbook I was touched to find a number of photographs of me and my brother. Beyond that, we had a common passion for the *Manchester Guardian* crossword and a shared sense of the ridiculous that from time to time gave us wonderful laughs together, so that what she was saying to me from her grave was plain enough. She was saying that I had never realized how my neglect all those years had hurt and offended her, and that was why it was only over her dead body that the family annals had come to me at last. And she was right. I had never fully realized it, and when at last I did, I also realized with a pang how sad it was that the old ghosts and griefs had kept us apart. There was so much we could have learned from each other, so many ways we could have been a comfort to each other and helped each other's healing. We could have been such friends.

The other voice that spoke to me through the discovery of the old book was my grandmother's. What absorbed me first, of course, was all the things that were in it, some of them more or less familiar and others that took me by surprise, like a piece from the *Brooklyn Eagle* describing how one summer day in 1907 my grandfather saved a man and his wife from drowning when their boat capsized in the combers off Rockaway Point where he and some friends were trolling for bluefish. But then what came to absorb me still more was what it suddenly occurred to me was *not* in it.

When my first novel, *A Long Day's Dying*, came out in 1950, it created more of a stir than anything I have ever done since. It got long, enthusiastic reviews not only in the *New York Times* and *Tribune*, but in countless other papers all over the country, not to mention magazines like *Time*, *Newsweek*, *The Saturday Review*, and so on. The dust-jacket photograph that Jimmy Merrill had taken of me outside our house in Georgetown showed up everywhere, and there was another picture in *Life*, which ran a story about me and several other young writers, among whom, I think I remember, were Paul Bowles and Brendan Gill. There were constant ads in the *New Yorker* and elsewhere, and for weeks I was even for the first and only time in my life on the best-seller list. For a few months, in other words, I was even more famous than Herman Balthasar Scharmann, and yet what I suddenly realized was that there was not a single clipping about it anywhere in all those gummed pages. What I realized next was why. Decades after her death, it was as if my grandmother herself was explaining it to me. The novel's dedication was why. It read, "For Naya, with love and wonder."

My grandmother Buechner was the one who had kept us afloat after my father's death because by then my grandfather Kuhn had lost all his money. It was she who had paid the rent, paid for our clothes, our car, school for Jamie and me, everything, yet the grandmother I dedicated my book to was the other one. Naya was the one I loved as much as I have ever loved anybody in my life—the teller of wonderful tales, the urbane and silver-tongued, who was the only one in the family to encourage my writing, the one whose serene and reassuring presence helped me believe as a child that even if the world I knew split in two beneath my feet, as long as she was around all would be well.

So what can I say to Grandma Buechner? You were such a force to be reckoned with, my dear. You were so fierce in your honesty, so frightening in your power, so demanding in your devotion, so overwhelmingly generous that I never knew how to thank you. But I loved you too. I loved you for having survived horrors that would have turned another heart to stone. I loved you for that moment in the dusk when on the far side of tears we met beyond where words alone could have taken us. I loved you for a strength that helped make me strong even though I had no idea of it at the time. And now I love you for having kept from me the hurt that I would never have known about if the family annals hadn't spilled the beans at last.

four

The half of the library you enter first is where the biographies are, together with some of the children's books—the Uncle Wiggilys, MacDonald, Tolkien, E. B. White, Kenneth Grahame. European fiction is there too and a few shelves of drama. In the history section there are a number of the books I used when I was writing *Godric* and *Brendan* and trying to get some feel for how people lived and thought in twelfth-century England for the first of them and sixth-century Ireland for the second. The largest section, most of one long wall, is devoted to religion—theology, church history, biblical studies, mysticism, saints' lives, and the like—and in the shelf that juts out at right angles from it, which together with the one on the other side divides the back half of the library from the front, there are my Buddhist books, many of them paperbacks which, when I was at Exeter, I had bound in saffron because that is the color of the fruit when it is ready to fall from the tree and thus for

Buddhism the holy color, signifying the process of falling at last from the world of suffering and ignorance into the bliss of nirvana.

Any minister's religion books reveal at a glance when he was at seminary, and mine include Karl Barth, of course, who was one of the great luminaries in my day at Union in New York. *The Word of God and the Word of Man* still moves me after all these years with its picture of people coming to church Sunday after Sunday with a single great question so deep in their hearts that sometimes they are hardly even aware of it. "*Is it true,*" he writes, "this talk of a loving and good God, who is more than one of the friendly idols whose rise is so easy to account for, and whose dominion is so brief? What the people want to find out and thoroughly understand is, *Is it true?* . . . They want to find out and thoroughly understand the answer to this one question, and not some answer that beats about the bush." I don't believe I have ever written a sermon without thinking about that question or have ever taken it for granted that even the most devout and committed congregations have already answered it to their satisfaction once and for all. In all my sermons as well as in all my books, fiction and nonfiction alike, I have always tried to address it as honestly and searchingly as I know how, because it is of course my question as well as everybody else's.

Tillich and Niebuhr are on my shelves too, both of them my teachers at Union—Niebuhr with his speech slightly slurred from a stroke but otherwise in no way diminished and Tillich with his lovely grandfatherly face and musical-comedy German pronunciation—but I was too in awe of them ever to speak so much as a word in their presence except once when I found myself alone with Tillich in an elevator and ventured some observation about the weather. Pedersen's great work on the life and culture of ancient Israel is there too, with its insights into the biblical understanding of such matters as names, blessing, blood, remembering, and death. "The world which lies in the sun, where men are moving and working, is the land of life," he writes. "Below it extends the land of death, Sheol. The dead dwell in the grave. But the individual grave is not an isolated world; it forms a whole with the graves of the kinsmen who make a common world and are closely united. Nor does the thought stop at this totality. Viewed from the world of light, all the deceased form a common realm." I think of how Naya answered me when I asked her if she had seen my father.

There are recent works as well, and none I value more than Marcus Borg's *Meeting Jesus Again for the First Time*. It was in church last Easter that the preacher, a good and intelligent man, looked out at his congregation toward the start of his sermon and asked if there were any of us there who weren't ashamed of our lives, and I wanted to hurl him bodily out of his pulpit and put Borg there instead. I wanted Borg to explain how for centuries the church has drawn its imagery so almost exclusively from what he calls "the priestly story" that it has all but forgotten the other two "macro-stories" that shape the Bible as a whole and depict the religious life in different ways. In the priestly story, we are depicted primarily as sinners who have good reason to be ashamed of our lives, and the religious life becomes a story of guilt, sacrifice, and God's forgiveness. Who can deny the moments when we recognize that as the story of all of us? And yet who can deny either that it is the story the church pushes because it is the church that is the official conveyer of God's forgiveness and presides over the eucharistic sacrifice? But on Easter Sunday, of all days, why not speak to us for a change in terms of one of the other two great stories, the Exodus, for instance, and ask us not if we are ashamed of our lives, but if we do not recognize in our lives all the ways that, like Israel, we too are in bondage, if only to our own shadows and shallowness, and need above all things not to be forgiven, but to be set free? Or why not remind us of the Exile story and ask if there are any of us who do not feel the sadness and loneliness and lostness of being separated from where we know in our hearts we truly belong, even if we're not sure either where it is to be found or how to get there, if there are any of us who do not yearn, more than for anything else, to go home. I remember a friend of mine saying once that she wished she could find a church where they didn't spend so much time apologizing. "Either instead of or alternating with the confession of sin," Borg writes, "what if we were to say, 'We are Pharaoh's slaves in Egypt, and we beseech you for liberation'? Or 'We live in Babylon, and we ask you for deliverance'?"

In the middle of this inner half of the library there is a maple drop-leaf table with both leaves extended and a chair at either side. On it there is a tall brass lamp that my daughter Dinah gave me with two slender necks arching gracefully downward like flowers, one to the left and one to the right, and ending in green glass shades. Naya has turned one of them on so that she can see the cards spread out on the table in front of her.

"At the original Canfield's, you paid fifty dollars for the pack," she says, "and they gave you five dollars back for each card you managed to play off on an ace. So far I am doing quite well, but of course I cheat. You're supposed to go through the pack one at a time only once, but I go through it in threes, shuffling each time, until there's not another card I can play. It seems irreverent to be gambling surrounded by all these books about God. I hope he won't mind."

There is something of Rembrandt in the way the light of the lamp has caught her face, her glasses, the table's surface, with the rest of the room in shadow.

"I don't remember that you and I ever talked much about God," I say, "but I remember that winter in Tryon when we used to go to the Episcopal church on Melrose Avenue together. It was before I went away to school."

"I'm afraid we went mainly to hear Harold Crandall in the choir," she says. "When they sang the Benedicite, he always took the solo part in his anguished, throbbing baritone—'O ye Lightnings and Clouds, bless ye the Lord. O ye whales and all that dwell in the waters, bless ye the Lord.' O ye this, that, and the other like the foghorn off Machias, and everybody else chiming in with 'Praise him and magnify him forever.' It gave us ungodly joy."

"Would you say you were a believer in those days?" I ask. She has a single card by one corner, a red queen, and is holding it hesitantly over the table looking for a place to play it.

"I was a Unitarian as much as I was anything," she says. "I believed in 'the achieving power of hopeful thought,' that lovely phrase. William Ellery Channing said it, I think. Or perhaps it was Mr. Emerson. I always believed too that there was more than met the eye."

"And how about now?" I ask.

Finding no place for the red queen, she replaces it among the cards in her hand and sets them softly down on the table.

"Well, the mystery is by no means solved, if that's what you think," she says. "On the contrary. I always felt quite at sea about it when I was on your side of things and never dwelt on it especially because there was so much else that seemed more pressing. I always assumed that when you died, you would no longer see through a glass darkly but face to face as St. Paul quite inaccurately predicted. However, such was not the case. On the contrary, it was like stepping out of a dark house into the greater dark of night."

She pauses for a moment, glancing up into the shadows as though they are the sky. One lens of her glasses catches the lamp's light.

"The moon," she says. "The Milky Way unwinding like a scarf, the constellations. All those fathoms upon fathoms of darkness. Who knows what other moons and stars there are farther still. What deeper depths.

"You'd think it would quite take your breath away, if you had breath to take," she says. "But it doesn't, *mirabile dictu*. It's almost as if it *is* your breath." She glances down at the pattern of cards on the table for a moment. "Or as if it's breathing you."

She gathers the lot of them into a single pile then and starts arranging them so that they all face the same way. Making them into a pack, she taps it lightly on the table to square it.

There is only one window in this end of the library, and it is behind Naya's chair. Through it I can see a patch of lawn and an apple tree, beyond that the horse pasture sloping gradually up to the top of the hill where the house stands that we lived in for some thirty years before moving down to the one that belonged to my wife's parents. Until we took it over, the house on the hill was the guest house, and now it is the guest house again, the place where our daughters stay when they come with their husbands and children. On the windowsill there are several objects—a black wrought-iron bank in the shape of a dachshund, a shoeshine parlor's brass footstand as delicately curved as a Brancusi, a jester's wand with a puffy face in the middle of a five-pointed silver star hung with lavender ribbons and one tiny remaining bell that tinkles if you shake it. On top of the lower sash is a wide band of plaited straw that came from Mexico, I think. It is the Last Supper with the flattened heads of the disciples, six on one side and six on the other, and another head in the middle that you know is Jesus because of the straw cross behind it.

"Tell me about Jesus," I say.

Behind her, through the window, I can see a chestnut mare at the pasture fence. She is nibbling at the grass with a white blaze on her nose. Every now and then she sweeps her satiny flanks with her tail. The lower part of her hind legs is obscured by the plaited straw.

"There was a poem about him I loved," she says. "I can't quite bring it back, but I can hear the music of it as clearly as your voice. Da da *dum*, da da *dum*." With one finger she taps it out lightly on the edge of the table.

"You will know him when he comes
Not by the roll of drums
Or the clarion trumpet's blare . . .

"That's not it, but short, solemn lines like that, not unlike drumbeats themselves. The idea is you will know him when he comes not by any outward show but—oh, dear—by his something kingly tread, in some quiet inner way. Maybe it will come back to me. As a Unitarian I didn't believe in his divinity, whatever exactly that means—being of one substance with the Father and all that—but I believed what the poem says. I believed I would know him if I ever saw him, even if he was just walking down Trade Street in the rain or standing behind the counter at Ballenger's. And I believe it still."

"You haven't seen him then?"

The little straw heads on the windowsill are faceless. They are sitting with their folded arms on the table, the one in the middle leaning ever so slightly to his right. The silvery light from the window shines through the straw.

"I will know him if I do," she says. And before I know that I am going to do it, I say, "He will know you."

"Who can tell?" she says. "Sometimes when you're going someplace, you send a scrap of your heart ahead. Isn't that what you taped on the back of your little heart-shaped stone? Maybe that scrap of mine is what he will know me by. 'There are more things in heaven and earth, Horatio.' Maybe I will know him because he sent me a scrap of his."

From time to time over the years people have asked me if I've ever thought of writing a novel about Jesus, and my answer always has been that I would no sooner write a novel about him than I would about anybody else I loved, such as my family, for instance, because to put words in their mouths and ascribe feelings to their hearts and try to imagine their inner lives would be to cheapen and somehow dishonor the bond between us. Another reason I would never write a novel about him is my fear of making his world, and him in it, as stagy and unconvincing as the color illustrations you find in inexpensive gift editions of the Bible. When I wrote *The Son of Laughter*, a novel about the biblical Jacob, I found that after a certain amount of digging around in books like Doughty's *Travels in Arabia Deserta* and Raphael Patai's *Sex and Family in the Bible and the Middle East* I got enough of a feeling for what it must have been like to live in the Bronze Age to be able to describe it with some sense that I might be getting it more or less right. But even though I have done a lot of the same kind of reading about the first-century world of Jesus, when it comes to writing about it, in sermons or anywhere else, I always have the sense that what I am describing is less the way it really was than the way I have seen it portrayed in those same unfortunate illustrations or their counterparts in movies, paintings, or other people's novels.

All this notwithstanding, I did once try off and on over the course of several years to write a novel about Mary Magdalen. I was fascinated by the tradition that she and the apostle John in their old age lived together in Ephesus and that at some earlier period the Virgin Mary had lived with them. I decided to have Mary Magdalen herself—Lena as she is called in the book—narrate the story and opened it with her description of herself and John—whom she calls "Thunder" after Jesus' sobriquet—as they make their way from their house in the hills down into the ancient city.

"Sometimes even Thunder has to laugh at how we stagger and slip on the loose stones as we go," I wrote. "If you didn't know he was laughing, you would think he was choking on a bone. With his stick in one hand, he clings so tight to me with the other that we become some four-legged monster cackling down the mountainside to hurl itself into the blue harbor. Thunder's broken nose veers off to one side, his cheeks full of shadow, his eyes staring and bright as a gull's in their deep sockets. My face is all folds and wrinkles like clothing hung out to dry and my hair every which way, but I have my teeth still, my body still slender. In a rare moment of tenderness, Thunder told me once that my smile is still foolish and bold as the smile of the girl I was when he knew me first.

"We buy fish in the city. We haggle over olives and wine, barley meal, figs, oil and the like at the peddlers' stalls, but mostly it's just for the sake of once in a while being part of the reeking, clamorous life of the place that we make the terrible climb down and then up again even though it's a life that so appalls Thunder that much of the time he pulls his cloak up over his head so he won't be turned to stone by the sight of it. He pulls it over his head when we pass by the young men wrestling and racing and playing at their games in the broad court by the public baths. They are as proud of their oiled and ringleted nakedness as Thunder is driven to fits by it. As for me, I am stirred by it. I am as far past desiring them as I am past their finding me desirable, but they are no less fair to my eyes than the circling of white birds or the shimmer of water on the hulls of the ships tied up at the wharves.

"Every day there are processions down the marble street with the statues of gods and emperors carried shoulder high to the throbbing of cymbals and drums and the keening of horns as they make their way past the terraced houses of the rich with their red tiled roofs, past the brothels, the public latrines, the shops and warehouses and colonnaded galleries where people of a hundred different tongues gather for shelter from the flaming sun.

"At the cypress gates of the Great Tart's temple, tattooed wizards hawk their philtres, spells, horoscopes, not to mention the small silver images of the towering, many-teated abomination inside that is said to have fallen out of the sky which must have bade it good riddance. Romans, Greeks, Jews, all mingle and jostle and trade there. Thunder calls the Romans Pigs because they have swilled down the world, and the Greeks Foxes because their speech can make as many feints and turns as a fox before its pursuers. I call the Jews goats in honor of their beards and their stubbornness and because the narrow slits of a goat's eye see no more of the world than the Jews see of truth. Even when truth stands before them with its eyes swollen shut and a broken jaw."

The characters of Lena and Thunder came increasingly alive to me as I explored them. I began to be able to see them, to hear their voices, to imagine my way inside their skins, until it gradually became a matter less of dreaming up words for them to speak and things for them to do than of simply sitting back and listening to what they were saying and watching to see what they would do next. Gradually too I began to have a feeling for Ephesus to the point where I could smell its smells a little—the sea air from the harbor, the offal in the streets, the flower markets and latrines, fish frying in oil over charcoal fires—and hear the clamor of it, watch the crowds of pilgrims, peddlers, shysters, at the gates of the temple of Diana. But what haunted me most, of course, was the thought of what memories Lena and Thunder must have shared of earlier days.

They were memories mainly of Jesus, of course, and they were what one way or another my novel would be about. My idea was never to try presenting him as he really existed in history, but only as he existed in their hearts a great many years later. I would never describe scenes from his life as they might actually have happened or words from his lips as he actually spoke them, but only their memories of those scenes and words. I ascribed to Lena herself both my own refusal to deal with him in any other way and also my own reasons for refusing. At one point in the novel she describes how year after year people from all over the Mediterranean world come seeking her and Thunder out in their house in Ephesus to ply them with questions about him—some because they are true believers, others simply because they are curious—and how she answers them.

"I tell them when he was alive he looked like a living man," she says, "and when he was dead like a dead man. I do not tell them what he looked like the last time my eyes saw him. How could I tell it?

"I do not tell of his feet, but only of the print of his feet in the dust. I do not tell of the look of him, but only of the look of the shadow he cast. I do not tell of the sound of his voice as he spoke, but only of the silence that followed in the wake of his speaking.

"I do not say his name because I never knew it, his true and secret name. I knew only the name that if you called it out would make him turn to see what you wanted the way he always turned to see what I wanted when I called it.

"I do not tell of the words I heard him speak, because on my lips they would no longer be his words. Nor do I tell anything about the meaning of his words or about what lay in his heart as he spoke them. Who knows what he meant? Who knows about his heart?

"If I were to paint on the wall a picture of his life, I would put in the sea, the villages, the paths and pathless hills and lowlands we traveled with him. I would put in the slow, brown river, the wedding, the fishermen friends and the storm, the little scoundrel in the tree. I would put in the lady his mother. I would put in the one he called the Rock with his brawn and bluster. I would put in the treasurer with his eyes flat and bright as coins.

"But where you might expect to find him himself, I would leave the wall bare and unpainted. At the center of the picture there would be an empty place, and the shape of the empty place would be the shape of my life without him."

It seemed to me a potentially moving and effective way to write a novel about Jesus without making him a character in it, but after a hundred pages or so, I could see it wasn't working. I didn't want to try to imagine how he really was because that would be to reduce him to no more than a figment of my imagination, and yet to have him absent from the book except as other people remembered him reduced him to almost less even than that. I felt increasingly frustrated by the restrictions I had placed on myself. When I described Lena's memories of scenes like the wedding at Cana or the dinner at the house of Simon the Pharisee with Jesus there only as a presence she felt too precious or painful to talk about, I felt stifled and depressed at not being able to talk about him either. So after several years of setting it aside to write something else instead and then picking it up again to see if this time I could somehow make it work, I finally decided to set it aside for good.

At some level, I suppose, it all had to do with my father. Maybe my not being able to remember him has some element in it of not wanting, like Lena, to reawaken memories too precious or painful to handle. Maybe my failure to find out much about him from other people's memories is related to my failure to find what I hoped for in the memories of Lena and Thunder. Maybe I remember so little about him simply because, for the ten years I knew him, he was hardly part of my childhood at all, but only the empty place at its center.

He was away all day working at whatever job he had at the time or away somewhere looking for another or trying to locate a place for us to live if he found one, and even when he was at home—evenings or weekends—I have only a meager handful of recollections. He went to the doctor's with me to have my arm set when I fell and fractured it. He taught me to ride a bike. He told me that to sleep with two pillows would make me round-shouldered. Otherwise I have virtually nothing left of him, and once in the midst of an unprecedented speech my mother commented on this and a number of other matters I had never known her to touch on before.

She was eighty-six years old at the time and not yet as crippled by her arthritic knees as she later became. The scene took place in her bedroom with the background sound of the maid vacuuming in the living room. I was sitting in the over-stuffed armchair where she spent much of her time those days, and she was standing at the foot of one of the twin beds, when without warning she launched into an extraordinary aria that must have lasted a good half an hour. Usually she closed her eyes when she spoke, but on this occasion I seem to remember they were wide open the whole time. Her subject was her marriage to my father, and she told me things that she had never told me before and never alluded to again. She spoke matter-of-factly, without any trace of emotion, and with no apparent ax to grind. I had the sense not so much that she was telling me things she wanted me to know, or knew that I wanted to hear, as that she was telling them simply because the time had come and they were things that after some fifty years of silence she needed to set before herself like Naya laying out her cards on the library table. I had the feeling that if I had not been there to listen, she might have told them to the empty chair.

It was all so epoch-making that I tried to summarize it later that same day and eventually copied the summary into my journal, where I refer to my mother as Kaki, her childhood name, which was later adopted by her three granddaughters and eventually by my brother and me and our wives.

"They were married 14 years, she said, of which the first 5 were happy and the next 9 not happy at all. He had much more of a drinking problem than I had realized, though only at parties, she said, not at home. Would become excessively talkative, amorous, was sexually aroused dancing with other women. While they were still living in NYC he came home from work after a bad day, opened the window and threatened to jump. Kaki called Grandma, who was at first annoyed to be bothered, then sent Grandpa B over, who put his arm around Daddy's shoulder and somehow jollied him out of it. Could this be the glimpse memory I have of him coming home one evening when I was on the floor in my room playing with blocks [they were wooden blocks sanded smooth as satin and painted blue] and feeling his face clammy and cold when he kissed me and knowing something was badly wrong?

"We children, Jamie and I, never seemed terribly important in his life, she said when I asked her. He loved us, was proud of having 2 sons, but never made a great deal of us.

"It was George Merck [whose daughter Judith I married in 1956] who asked Kaki to come see him when he was recovering from pneumonia and urged her to get him to a psychiatrist (whose name I think was Cheney; K didn't remember it). K took him to his office where there was some poor soul all bent over and mad, and she said to D she hoped he wouldn't become like that and had always regretted saying it. The psychiatrist said she was to blame for his condition (could he really have said it?), and K said she shd. meet his mother who was always threatening to put her head in the gas oven to escape her own sad marriage. K almost, *almost*, gave me back a memory then when she said he went for a week or so to some neurological institute where she took Jamie and me to visit him. I grasped out for the memory and just failed to get hold of it. They had taken his necktie, razor etc. away. He had a roommate [the roommate is part of what I thought I could all but remember, grey-haired, soft-looking]. He spent much of the visit showing us photos of the roommate's children, paying relatively little attention to his own. Did he? Did he? I almost remember something of it.

"He kept losing jobs, kept going to people like Aunt Tony Liebmann [one of my grandmother Buechner's four sisters] and the Zinsser cousins to give him an allowance till he found work again. His Princeton roommate Sam Kauffman gave him what was apparently quite a menial job on the *Washington Evening Star*. It had something to do with circulation. He would drive around the Virginia countryside checking to see if the paper was put in the tubular holders. Sometimes he took us. Again I can *almost* remember.

"He and Kaki both, I guess, 'played around.' He took some girl to Grandma's empty apartment. He encouraged Kaki's affair with one of their friends. When the friend would come to supper in Essex Fells, Daddy would say he was tired and had to go to bed and asked him to entertain her. Then the friend would hug and kiss her, she said, or something like that. After the neurological institute Daddy and Uncle Rob [his younger brother] took a little trip together to Hot Springs, Virginia, where D wrote Kaki a letter saying something like 'I wish I were here with you,' and Kaki said she'd always wished she kept it.

"Details of suicide. Just Grandma and I were to go with him to the football game that Saturday. Jamie was too young and Kaki was going to stay with him. Kaki was awakened by the black butler (John?). She and Gma went down to the garage where they found him slumped on the running board of the car. They tried to chafe his wrists. Kaki could tell from his hands that he was dead.

"'Everybody came,' she said. Uncle Rob, the Wicks [her sister, Ruth, and her husband], I guess Uncle Tom. The Wicks took us to Greenwich. Gma and Aunt Betty took K to the movies later, and in the midst of it K started crying and couldn't stop.

"Drunk, Daddy once threw her down the hall in front of Mrs. Taylor, our nurse. Parked the car across the streetcar tracks in Georgetown [Washington] and K had to push it off somehow.

"The psych. or neurolog. inst. diagnosed him as manic depressive. Kaki vague about what they did or recommended.

"It was an extraordinary speech—I sitting in a chair in K's bedroom (maid working in liv. rm.) and K standing talking to me, her eyes closed [closed? open?]. She talked, and I listened, without emotion. When she finished, she said. 'I hope these horrible things won't take your appetite away.' I more or less laughed and said of course not, and we went in to the chicken salad the maid had prepared. Two old conspirators, years after the success of their conspiracy?

"She told me some weeks later that she told Jamie many of the same things and suddenly saw he was crying."

In the office, where the computer is, and the copier, the fax machine, the two-tiered wire basket of unanswered letters, there are a number of things hanging on the walls, among them an old Vermont license plate bearing the single word TRUST, a photograph some reader sent me of St. John's Chapel at the Tower of London, and a parchment document lettered in gold ink by my Charlotte, North Carolina, friends Goldie Stribling and Betty McLaney which reads, "St. Godric's Day / 21 May 1981 / On the feast day / of / Saint Godric of Finchale, / we do humbly offer thanks / for his pilgrimage / and the grand company / of friends along his way / For his humanity, humility / and holiness / And for his re-creator / our mentor and friend / Amen and Amen." On another wall there is a head-and-shoulders photograph of Jimmy looking as wrinkled as an old marmoset with a good-for-nothing, sleepy-eyed grin on his face and his head tilted sideways so that it almost touches what is either a stemmed glass vase or a large brandy snifter. Two framed certificates of American citizenship hang one above the other. One of them bears the name of my great-grandfather August Büchner, the umlaut still intact, dated 1875, and the other of his wife, Charlotte Elizabeth, dated 1864. There is a black-and-white photograph I once took of Rosa and Anna Pelkoffer, the German sisters who worked for Grandma Buechner from my father's childhood on into my young manhood. They are standing side by side in the kitchen holding between them our dachshund Hansi, whom they took care of for us during his later years. He was apparently with my father in the garage that fatal November morning but lived to tell the tale, maybe because he was built so close to the ground that he was below the level of danger.

On the wall facing me when I sit at my desk—underneath two shelves of reference books—is a copy of Rembrandt's etching "The Return of the Prodigal Son" signed and dated by him 1636. The Prodigal, naked except for a breechcloth, is kneeling on the topmost stone step leading to an open door. His raised hands are clasped at his lips. His father in a long-sleeved cloak and turban has bent over to embrace him, one hand resting on his bare shoulder, the other reaching down to support him under the forearm. The father's eyes are closed and his brow furrowed. The Prodigal's eyes are open. His hair is tangled, and he has a ravaged, vulpine face. You can imagine him curled up at night on a hot-air grating. There is an air of exhaustion about him, but in his father's arms you can see he has come home. It hardly matters which is the father and which the son.

They have both come home.

five

Sick with anxiety, depressed, doom-ridden, I was parked once in front of Peltier's market in Dorset, Vermont, when I spotted a car coming south on Route 30 with the license plate that now hangs on my office wall. TRUST, it said, the one word of all words that at that moment I needed most to hear. Below it hangs the photograph of St. John's Chapel, above it the photograph of a black African Christ carved in wood.

It was several years later that the owner of the plate, a stranger, turned up at our house one day and handed it to me. He'd read my description of the incident somewhere and thought I would like to have it, even though by then it was considerably the worse for wear, with crumpled edges, the green paint rusted off in places, and the registration sticker in one corner all but illegible. He was, as I had guessed, the trust officer in a bank. He was also the unwitting bearer to me not only of that one word of all words, but of the message that, tortuous though our paths through the world are, I was nonetheless by some miracle where I was supposed to be. I had turned up at the right place at the right time. I had been expected.

The heart-shaped stone wedged into the crevice of rock where I stepped ashore on the island of Outer Farne in the North Sea bore the same message, and there on the windowsill near a miniature replica of Dorothy's ruby slippers and a tiny brass statuette of Harry Truman in a double-breasted suit and spectacles, it bears it still.

Last fall my wife and I went to Greece for the first time. Everybody told us that if we saw nothing else, we must be sure to see Delphi, and it was good advice. First, however, we saw Athens, where for years Jimmy had a house that because of some exchange problem, he told me, he had paid for with a bag of gold and that, to his amusement, was located on the street of the Athenian Ephebes. The air was so full of exhaust fumes that my eyes stung and watered for as long as we were there, and many of the streets were torn up where for years they have been trying to install a subway system. Our driver, Strato—a beguiling, voluble young man who said he felt "honored" by my attempts to recapture what little Greek I still remembered and had a daughter with the name of Evangelia—was the one who explained that the process was endless because every time you dig a hole in Athens, you come upon treasures and the archaeologists have to be summoned. Strato was also the one who drove us to Delphi, a long, not very interesting trip until Mt. Parnassus begins to come into view and you finally find your way to the Sanctuary of Apollo on its slopes. The view is of the deep Pleistos river valley with its silvery grey sea of olive trees and beyond it the Gulf of Corinth shining in the light. Birds wheel though the air below you, and you can sense the presence of the gods everywhere. "Even now an aura of mystery invests the sparse ruins," the Michelin guide reads, and it is true.

Above what remains of the Temple of Apollo—a few columns still standing, the flagged pavement, the fallen stones—there are the ruins of the stadium where the Pythian games once took place. I had wandered there by myself and was on my way back down the steep dirt path when I heard a woman's voice behind me somewhere say, "Is it very hard?" Assuming she must be talking to someone else, I continued on my way until something made me stop and turn. It was an American woman who had spoken. She was leaning against the bank a few yards above me on the path, a camera strung around her neck. She was on the heavy side with dyed black hair, and when I asked her if I was the one she had been addressing, she said I was. She had simply wondered if it was a hard climb up to the stadium, she explained, and I told her it wasn't bad. The path flattened out just beyond the next bend. "Not as hard as Mt. Olympus then?" she said, and I told her I had never been to Mt. Olympus.

That was the entire extent of our conversation, and it wasn't until I heard myself describing it to my wife and our friends a few minutes later that I realized what had happened. The gods were famous for assuming human form, I told them, and I had just been talking to one of them. It might have been Athena or her half sister Artemis, Apollo's twin. Possibly it was the Oracle herself. I could see they all but believed me. I all but believed myself.

As to what happened at the Temple of Poseidon at Sounion a few days later, there could be no doubt. Strato drove us there too, promising to take us to a restaurant run by three brothers of his acquaintance on the way back. He said he would drink iced coffee while we inspected the famous ruins, and we were not to hurry on his account. For as long as we were paying him, he explained, he belonged entirely to us. The temple stood on a precipitous headland looking over the Aegean Sea at the entrance to the Saronic Gulf and out toward the Cyclades. According to Michelin, we read, Lord Byron visited it in 1810 and carved his name on one of the four corner pillars that still remain standing. We were never able to find it, but what I found instead were the first four letters of my name—BUEC— deeply cut into the base of one of the pillars. Again I had apparently been expected.

For some years now we have gone to Switzerland once or twice a year because our daughter Dinah lives there with her husband and two small sons, and one summer we stayed with them for a few days in Klosters, where the alps glitter in the distance, and the cows, their great bells randomly chiming, graze on close-cropped green meadows that rise into the sky. Here and there narrow paths wind their way parallel to the road below, and we were walking along one of them one morning with Dinah and her two little boys, the younger in a stroller, when we came to a hay shed, low-roofed and wooden, that looked straight out of *Heidi*. We paused at it for a moment, and I noticed that somebody had scratched something on one side of it with a bottle cap maybe or a stone and wondered if it would be a Swiss version of the crudities you would expect to find at home. The letters were hard to read, and it took a little time to make them out. *Gott heisst Lieben und Leben* was what somebody had written there, the words chiming like cowbells, fragrant as hay, serene and transcendent as the snow-capped mountains.

Trust says the crumpled green license plate that hangs in my office. Trust what? Trust that it is worth scratching on the wall that God Is Love and Life because, all appearances to the contrary notwithstanding, it may just be true. Trust that if God is anywhere, God is here, which means that there is no telling where God may turn up next—around what sudden bend of the path if you happen to have your eyes and ears open, your wits about you, in what odd, small moments almost too foolish to tell. If God is ever, God is now, in the in and out of breathing, the sound of the footstep on the stair, the smell of the rain, the touch of a hand on your bare shoulder where you kneel at the door. If God lives and loves, as the hay shed proclaimed, it is in ourselves no less than everywhere else, in the godless no less than the godliest, in the dead no less than the living, because the end of a life is no more likely to be the end of God's love that keeps it alive than it is of our love that keeps it a living part of ourselves the way Naya remains as much a part of me as she was before that night in her ninety-fourth year when the Toonerville Trolley of the world slowed down enough for her to dismount at last.

Will I remain on the trolleycar long enough to become part of my grandchildren's lives the same way, those six small boys and that one even smaller girl born only a few weeks ago? I am already part at least of the boys' lives—they remember books we've read together and places we've gone, they seem glad to see me when I turn up, we have private jokes—but how long will it continue? My father must have been part of my life for the ten years I knew him, but within a short time of his death I forgot almost everything about him I had once known. And yet years before I ever saw his signature, I started writing the capital *F* of my first name backwards the way he did and who knows what else of me is from him too.

One summer before I was married, I rented a house in Maine on the proceeds from my first novel, and one Sunday morning we were all sitting around in the living room—my brother and I together with our mother, Naya, and Uncle Jimmy Kuhn—when to our unmixed horror we spotted a small deputation coming up the front path obviously fresh from church with the woman in a white straw hat and white gloves and the two men in jackets and ties. We, on the other hand, had none of us been to church probably for years and couldn't have looked scruffier or more unpromising. In his pajamas, Uncle Jimmy, still bleary-eyed from sleep and unshaven, made a dash for the small bedroom off the living room where he was trapped, and the rest of us received the visitors with as much grace as we could muster. The woman in white gloves turned out to be named Edith King, a hitherto unknown second cousin of Naya's on her New England mother's side, who was interested in genealogy, and the two men were her husband and brother, neither of whom was interested in genealogy at all. It was clear they had both been dragged along against their better judgment.

When they left, perhaps an hour later, Uncle Jimmy, loping out of hiding to gibber around the living room like the family idiot we had locked away to avoid disgrace, occasioned such a wild burst of hilarity that the cousins, still within earshot, heard it, and Naya was horrified to get a letter from Edith King soon afterwards saying she knew they were a little odd but had not realized they were a three-ring circus. Naya wrote back explaining about Uncle Jimmy as best she could, and in time Edith and I became pen pals. Over the years she sent me a great deal of Poor, Porter, and Barton history that is now in the grey boxes of the family archives and shows among other things exactly how we are related to Clara Barton, for one, and to Rufus Porter, for another, itinerant muralist, inventor, and first editor of the *Scientific American*, who may have been the model for Mark Twain's Connecticut Yankee.

But the most remarkable part of the visit was that even the bored husband and brother got interested in spite of themselves. One or the other of them would point at one or the other of us and then all three would agree that whichever of us it was looked remarkably like some remote cousin we had never so much as heard of, let alone seen, and for the first time it occurred to me that there is no plumbing the mystery of genetics. Even if I'm not around long enough for my grandchildren to remember me, who knows in what way I may be part of them anyway? One of them may end up writing backward *F*'s like me and my father, or developing an inexplicable predilection for the Uncle Wiggily books, or having the little star-shaped dimple on the knuckle of the left thumb that I share with both Naya and my oldest daughter, Katherine. If they don't, maybe their children will or their children's children who knows how far away down the corridor of the years. My Leipzig-born great-grandfather, August Büchner, whose U.S. citizenship certificate hangs framed on the wall, was a bibliophile, book dealer, and archivist in New York City. Is it to him that I owe my taste for grey boxes? In one of them I have a photograph of him sitting with his wife and children in the garden of their gingerbread house at Fort Hill on Staten Island. His derby hat is at a rakish angle. He has a stylish beard and moustache and looks jaded and a little dissolute. Each family on earth is a magic kingdom, and the spells that it casts are long-lasting and powerful.

It was not in Klosters but in the village of Pratteln, across the Rhine from Basel, that I met the first of my grandsons for the first time. His name is Oliver. Dinah, his mother, had him in her arms as she came down the stairs to show him to us, and I went up the stairs to meet him halfway. He had flaxen hair and serene blue eyes. He looked straight at me and gave a faint smile.

I thought of how, only a few months old, he was on his way down into the world and I, sixty-seven years old, on my way up out of it. I thought of how when I am out of it altogether, he will carry my genes into times and places beyond my power to imagine and how he was now one of the few for whom—such is the mystery of kinship—I would lay down my life in ten seconds flat if it took that to save his. I thought of how, years after their deaths, he had made my mother a great-grandmother and my father a great-grandfather for the first time, as if they were still a going concern. Both of them were as remote from him as August Büchner in his derby hat from me, and yet he had given them new names and a small new heart for pumping something of their blood into the next millennium. Not long afterwards I preached at Westminster Abbey, of all places, and the proudest part of that proud moment for me was managing somehow to work his name, Oliver, into my sermon and in that haunted dusk describing our historic first encounter on the stairs.

It was to him and my other four grandsons up to that point that I dedicated a collection of short pieces called *The Longing for Home* in 1996: Benjamin, who, though he now takes us more or less in his stride, in his earlier days used to greet Judy and me with his head cocked sideways and an expression of such seraphic rapture that it was almost more than he could manage; and Dylan, inward-looking and full of secrets, who loves to be read to and of all of them reminds me most of myself as a child; and his younger brother, Tristan, with his snaggle-tooth smile who, when the Mouse King was run through by a sword in a high-school production of Tchaikovsky's *The Nutcracker*, electrified the entire audience by piping out in his needle-sharp treble, "The big rat is dead!"; and Oliver's younger brother, Brendan, the dreamer and goofball, who much of the time is lost in his own world but surfaces every now and then to run

up and say, "Alladee" or "Alladee-so," which, translated, means
"I love you more than words can tell." Since them, two others
have been born: Benjamin's brother, Noah, sleepy-eyed with a
laugh like a bass drum, and Caroline, about the size of a loaf of
bread, with a witty, intelligent little face as if she is concentrating on what she will say when the curtain rises at last.

Among the pieces in the book there is a group of thinly disguised family poems, the last of which is addressed to all seven
of them:

> Until I finished them, I didn't see
> that all these poems are yours. At best
> I thought they were a way for me
> once and for all to lay to rest
>
> this family, all but one of whom I've lost,
> with maybe a truth or two of who
> they were, like farewell flowers tossed
> into a grave. I never knew
>
> that all the while within my heart,
> unknowingly, I was in search of any
> way I could to bring some part
> of them to life so you, their children many
>
> times removed, might have a sense
> of how alive they were when I

first knew them as a child and hence
might even, as the years go by,

a little come to love them too.
If you could meet them, would they say,
as I suspect, that even though it's true
they knew much sadness in their day,

they're glad they lived at any cost?
That now at last they start to see
they've found more even than they lost?
Let it be so. Remember them for me.

"And I'm sure they will remember you too, dear lad," Naya says, "but it is a mixed blessing."

She is no longer in her eighties, but in her mid-fifties or so, gazing at me out of a silver frame on my desk. She looks very elegant, very patrician. The picture is dark with a string of pearls just visible, a deep fur collar that softens the line of her jaw. She is wearing a turban, her face half in shadow. She may not have given the portrait photographer the smile he asked for, but there is the faint prelude to one. She has something of Virginia Woolf in her deeply slanted brows and brave eyes, something of the last Tsarina.

"There aren't many left who remember me," she says. "For a long time the Grier sisters did, who lived to be a hundred or so and for all I know may still be going strong. Their house was behind ours on Woodland Road, and sometimes they used to bring me their French homework to help them with when they were children. There were also a few others I never would have thought I made much impression on like that lanky young Bob who used to produce our Cokes for us at Missildine's, and black Martha Dawkins who worked for your mother for a while. Once when a snake was discovered in the cellar, your mother made a dreadful row, and when she asked about it later, Martha fixed her with her bespectacled stare and announced simply, 'I took care of it.' That's all she would say on the subject, but the snake was never heard of again. Every time somebody like that remembers me, it's like a phone ringing I'm not sure just where, and sometimes I go see who it is and sometimes, I confess, I just let it ring till whoever it is starts thinking about something else instead."

"When I think about you," I say, "when I write about you like this, do you know about it somehow? Do you wish I'd let you be?"

Her face in the photograph seems to be looking directly at me now rather than slightly to the side. She has come a shade closer to smiling. There is something about her that reminds me a little of my daughter Katherine, who met her once when she was two and Naya ninety-four. The meeting took place in the small private nursing home in Tryon, where Naya's room looked out on the garden. It was rather shadowy, and Katherine had never seen anybody that old before. We lifted her up onto the bed, and she started crying when Naya reached out to touch her hand.

"There have been times I've glimpsed bits and pieces of things through your eyes," she says, "like your brown hand on the page of your notebook, for instance, or that apple branch outside your window now in the rain. Every once and again I've sensed you were near the way you sense somebody is when it's too dark to see the hand in front of your face, or too bright, I might better say, the way it is when the sun's in your eyes, the way it is here. It's not me you need to let be, dear boy. It's yourself. Let yourself be what you need to be most, and think about me as much as you please, or as little. It's true that a ringing phone can be a nuisance when you're trying to think long thoughts, but if it stopped ringing altogether, I suppose I might come to miss it."

"The last time I dreamed about you," I say, "we were crossing a street together in New York."

"The traffic was appalling," she says. "All those buses and cars and exorbitant yellow cabs. It was bad enough when there were only horses. I was glad to have your manly arm to cling on to. It reminded me of the days when you were a little boy in a beret and leggings and we used to inspect the trash cans set out on the sidewalk in front of brownstones when we took our walk, and if there were things like lobster shells or champagne bottles in them, we called it swell swill. Do you remember that, you with your penchant for the snows of yesteryear?"

"I remember you took me to call on a friend once, and I crawled in underneath a gate-leg table and couldn't get out, or was afraid to."

"It was my friend Isabelle McClung," she says. "She was the love of Willa Cather's life."

"Did you ever meet Willa Cather?"

"No, but I introduced Amy Lowell once when she lectured at the Twentieth Century in Pittsburgh. Later, when our chauffeur, who you may remember was wondrously named Gear, drove her down to the railway station in our car, she reclined in the back seat puffing on a big black cigar for all the world to see, and he nearly died of humiliation."

"What a long time ago that was," I say. "Another world."

"Leg over leg the dog went to Dover," she says. "If I had had a dollar for every time I heard your grandfather say that, I would have died a rich woman."

The photograph has a bit of the dark background torn away slightly above and to the right of Naya's head, but I put a piece of black construction paper behind it and you hardly notice. The silver frame was my mother's and is engraved on the left with the initials of her maiden name—K.K. She looked nothing like Naya as far as I could ever see except for maybe a little around the eyes. Maybe someday Caroline will.

In *Life, a User's Manual*, which Jimmy recommended to me the last time we really met, Georges Perec describes a tribe called the Kubus who had no more than a few dozen words in their language, leading him to wonder if "in the image of their distant neighbors the Papuans, [they] didn't voluntarily impoverish their vocabulary, deleting words each time a death occurred in the village." By the look of his photograph with bulging eyes, a billy-goat beard, and his hair flying, Perec was a raving maniac, but I know what he meant. Each time members of the tribe die, the self we were with them dies too, which is to say that the kind of words we spoke only to them—*were* only to them—and the kind they spoke only to us are spoken no longer. But if outwardly our language is thus impoverished, inwardly it is enriched because when members of the tribe die, the words they were are added to the vocabulary of the heart, where we have more than just ears for hearing them. And each time a member of the tribe is born, a new word comes into being, and nothing is ever the same again.

six

I wonder sometimes what will become of the Magic Kingdom after I've gone wherever it is we go, or maybe just out like a light as I suspect most of the people I know would bet if they had to. As for the family archives—the grey boxes, my father's baby book, the old photograph albums, the diaries I have been keeping for forty years or so, and the like—I have specified in my will that unless my children want to hold on to it all for some reason, I hope they will ship it out to the Wheaton College library in Illinois, where I'm told that for one purpose or another people turn up several times a month to look through the rather sizable collection of letters, manuscripts, and assorted papers that I have been giving them over the years including the copy of *Gone with the Wind* in which my father penciled his last few lines to my mother. I chose Wheaton rather than Princeton, my alma mater, for two reasons. One was that it has a unique collection of the papers of C. S. Lewis, George

Macdonald, J. R. R. Tolkien, and the like, and I could think of no more distinguished company for my literary remains to molder among, and the other was that for many years Princeton has so completely ignored me as a writer that when I wrote them years ago to ask if they would be interested in having my manuscripts, they didn't even answer the letter. When Jimmy's death precipitated a great burst of attention to him and his work, they suddenly had a change of heart. For years, they wrote, they had been of course very interested in me and my work and wondered now if I would consider giving them my correspondence with this most distinguished American poet, who they understood had been my close friend. I wrote back explaining why I wasn't inclined to give them so much as the time of day and then added that they reminded me of the real estate agents you read about who watch the obituary columns for a lead on a good apartment. I was tempted to add a comment on the name of the librarian who had written me, which was Skemer, but was able to resist it. They never answered.

One way or another, then, the family archives will be disposed of, but what about all those shelves upon shelves of books—*The Chronicles of Narnia*, the E. Nesbits, the Lang fairy-tale collections, all of them first editions? What about the copy of T. S. Eliot's poems and another of his essays both of which, when he lectured at Princeton my senior year, I stood in a queue for him to sign for me, watching him draw an elegant line through his name on the title page and write it out by hand just above as I have been doing it myself ever since? What about the lovely sixteen-volume set of Browning in dark blue leather, with the seal of King's College stamped in gold on all the spines and covers, which I discovered in Tunbridge Wells when Judy and I were in England for our honeymoon in 1956? I bought it from Mr. Pratley of Hall's Bookstore, which was so full of treasures in those days—one entire room filled almost entirely with seventeenth- and eighteenth-century volumes in their original bindings—that I kept returning to it in my dreams until years later when I went back to find that Mr. Pratley was long since gone and the magical room filled with nothing more exciting than the kind of used books you would be apt to find almost anywhere. What about the complete New York edition of Henry James including the posthumously printed volume 25 which was missing when I bought it but added when Tom and Kit Foster gave it to me from their broken set years later, or the three-volume Congreve with Anthony Trollope's crested bookplate in it? In acetate covers I've made to protect their wrappers, I have everything that William Maxwell has ever written including his long-out-of-print first novel, *Bright Center of Heaven*, published in 1934, which is so mannered and brittle and unconvincing that I can't imagine anyone's foreseeing that only three years later, in *They Came Like Swallows*, he would have found not only his own true voice but the truth of his own life, about which or out of which he has been writing ever since, one of the most neglected of all our great novelists. There are also all thirteen of the existing volumes of *The Yellow Book*, which I bought for twenty dollars when Jimmy and I were going through our Mauve Decade in the

1940s, and from about the same period a faded green copy-book whose front cover I had to mend where a dachshund of mine named Faustl chewed off the upper corner in my bachelor days. The book is entitled *Polaris*, and on facing pages Jimmy and I each wrote out the seven Lawrenceville poems we thought were our masterpieces. The foreword, in Jimmy's hand, reads in part, "This edition was limited to two copies because from those who have appreciated us and our poems, our enthusiasm alone has been great enough to merit the presentation of this book to each other."

Although my three daughters are all devoted readers, none of them has ever shown any particular interest in books as objects of veneration, and therefore I have thought about possibly leaving the collection to my grandchildren instead. For a while I fantasized about working out some sort of competitive examination that could be administered to them when they reach a certain age, with everything going to whoever gets the highest grade, but then one of my sons-in-law said that Sharmy's son Benjamin would undoubtedly win hands down, and that took the excitement out of it. So unless something else occurs to me, I will probably just decide to let fate take its course. John DeMarco, who owns the Lyrical Ballad Bookstore in Saratoga, did a detailed appraisal and catalogue for me a few years ago, and with that in hand, my heirs will learn, for instance, that the copy of *The Catcher in the Rye* is a first edition (so stated) in the first-issue dust jacket with Salinger's cow-eyed photograph on the back, which I paid thirty-five cents for at a college book sale around 1970 and which is currently going for about the price of a ticket to Europe on the *QE II.*

But the catalogue will tell them nothing about the real treasures. There is the large, fat folio, for instance, that I bound in red leather with my own hands under the close and skeptical supervision of my friend Posy Gerlach, who with her husband, Gerhart, was among the foremost binders in the country, and that contains, hinged to the pages with Japanese fiber paper, the two hundred or so surviving letters that Naya wrote me from 1929, when I was three and she going on sixty-three ("Dear Freddy Boy Bacon, I hear you have a new nurse and I hope you are a goody boy and go walking with her in the park and don't fuss and holler like a girl baby"), to the last, which she wrote within a few months of her death in June of 1961 when her writing was almost too shaky to decipher and which ends with a quotation she copied down in hopes that I might be able to identify it—"Beauty that must die and joy whose hand etc. etc."

On the bottom shelf, just to the right of the fireplace, there are two volumes having to do with Naya's father, Jules Golay, a Swiss from Geneva, and several shelves above them there is the shabby little black pocket edition of the French New Testament he carried with him in the Civil War. On the faded orange endpaper he has inscribed it "René D'Algers," his nom de guerre, "Front of Petersburg, August 28th, 1864," and it was at Petersburg, the longest and costliest siege in American warfare, that from a Southern sharpshooter he received the shoulder wound that eventually, sixteen years later, caused his death. On a table nearby there is also his small, square photograph album of nearly threadbare plum-colored velvet with the covers framed in brass and a brass medallion bearing his name and the year 1866 on the front. Is it possible that some grandchild will pick one or the other of these volumes up someday and wonder who he was? Maybe Oliver, who is half Swiss himself, will be the one. Maybe on some rainy afternoon when there isn't much else to do either he or his brother, Brendan, will get interested enough in their thrice-great-grandfather to go browsing through the grey box that bears his name. If so, they will find there his U.S. passport, which will tell them that in 1871, at the age of twenty-nine, he was five feet eight inches tall, had brown hair and dark eyes, and wore a beard. If they persist they will also come across his certificate of U.S. citizenship, a number of letters in his impeccable English, many of them unsuccessful attempts to get his government pension increased on the grounds that he was increasingly disabled by his wound, and his will. They may also find a letter from his first wife, Martha Osgood Poor, known as Mattie, Naya's mother, describing their marriage in her cousin Clara Barton's house in Washington, D.C., on Christmas Day, 1866, which was also Clara Barton's forty-fifth birthday. Writing to her Aunt Hannah Barton in Augusta, Maine, she says she will enclose two samples of material from her trousseau, and they are both still there in the envelope held together by a slightly rusty pin——one a piece of royal blue silk and the other a finely woven swatch of grey flannel.

If they search further through the grey box, they may come across a letter from Jules to the same Aunt Hannah, telling her that Mattie had died of consumption that summer. She was thirty-one years old when it happened and their baby daughter, Antoinette, who grew up to be Naya, was only eight months. Mattie died at the home of her Aunt Julia Barton in North Oxford, Massachusetts, where because of her bad health Jules had sent her and the baby while he stayed on in Washington, planning to come bring them home later. "They told me in Mass. that she had frequent hemorrhages through the summer [but] she was hopeful of recovery till the last minute and died very easily. I do not believe that she ever knew how near death she was." As for the baby, he went on, "It seems as if the darling little one knew that her mother was gone and she pined away till no one expected her to live and the doctor had given her up, but thanks to the good care of dear Aunt Julia she is much better and almost well." He announces his intention of bringing her back to be with him in Washington as soon as he can. She was a scrawny, dark little thing, apparently, who, according to Naya herself, was described by somebody at the time as looking like a spider in a saucer of milk.

It is in that bottom shelf near the fireplace, however, that the real prize is. Enclosed in the box Posy and I made for it, it is a limp-covered exercise book with faintly lined pages in which Jules Golay's second wife wrote in her strong, clear hand the story of his life. Her name was Harriet Chase Barrett, from Brewer, Maine, and as a child I knew her as Grammy. I remember the mingled sense of horror and wild exhilaration with which I dropped a plush monkey down on her head from the top of the three-story stairwell in Naya's house on Woodland Road. I remember her crying out in alarm when Uncle Jimmy Kuhn, her step-grandson, waltzed her around and around the carpeted hall in a fit of high spirits. I remember our parents driving Jamie and me up to Machiasport, Maine, for the occasion of her ninetieth birthday in the summer of 1935, and how impressed Daddy was by the number of ears of corn she managed to put away for a woman her age. I don't know at what point she wrote her life of the husband whom she survived by more than half a century, but it is a remarkable document, discerning, candid, and entirely unsentimental even when she is dealing with events that at the time must have been almost unbearable.

After a paragraph addressed to her children in which she explains that she is setting down their father's life because "I am the only one now living who can do this," she proceeds directly to his birth in Geneva on March 25, 1842, which she points out was Good Friday, and then says, "He was born with a caul which the midwife who attended his mother said showed that his life would be remarkable, but tho' his comparatively few years were full and busy ones and he was a man of more than common ability, his life was not remarkable." With these words she sets the stage for the story she has to tell.

There are pictures of both of his parents in the plum-colored album. His father, Isaac Golay, who was one of the oldest judges of the Superior Court of Geneva, is seated in a velvet-collared frock coat that looks several sizes too large for him, and his mother, born Rose Antoinette Besançon, after whom Naya was named, is also seated with her left arm resting on a little table with several books on it and her right fist clenched in her lap. According to Naya, who never met either of them, her grandmother was proud of her distinguished Huguenot descent and tended to remind her husband of it on appropriate occasions. She is wearing what must have been her best hoop-skirted, long-sleeved silk dress with a lace collar, a fancy little bonnet tied under her chin, and white lappets that fall down as far as her waist in front. Whereas her husband's expression, as befits a judge, is grave and thoughtful—he has heavy pouches under his eyes, and his mouth is set firm—she is glancing off sharply to one side, possibly at the person who has just told her to smile, which, in a sort of fierce, embarrassed way, she seems to be attempting. Her life was so busy supervising the women who worked downstairs in her husband's jewelry manufacturing business that when Jules was a baby she put him, the youngest of three, "out to be nursed by a woman in the country with whom and in whose family he spent several happy years," Grammy writes, "[crying] bitterly when his parents brought him back to their home in the city. They were almost strangers to him tho' they had from time to time gone to see him."

Years after his death when Clara Barton went to visit his parents in Geneva, she wrote a friend that she found "so good, kind and tender an old Papa I wonder he is permitted to stay here at all," but he must have mellowed with age by then, because Jules told Grammy that his childhood was not a happy one and recounted an incident she said she had always remembered. "There was company one evening and when he knew that his bedtime had come though childlike hating to leave the warm bright room with the eating and laughing of the guests, he got his little candle and standing by the door said in his best manner *'Bon nuit, Papa* [Grammy's French was as minimal as her punctuation]. *Bon nuit, Maman. Bon nuit tous le monde'* hoping to get some nod or look of commendation but his father and mother took no notice and only one or two of the guests gave him a careless *'Bon nuit.'* The poor little fellow took himself to bed alone and cried quietly at the disappointment and the feeling that no one cared for him."

Nevertheless he was given a good education both in Geneva and at some school in Germany—Grammy is vague about these early details—and somewhere along the line he ran away from home, either coming back on his own eventually or found and brought back by his father. In any case, he apparently left school early and got a job traveling for a firm of wine merchants who sent him, among other places, to Algiers, where he was when his father summoned him home to straighten out the money affairs of the jewelry business. His brother, Abraham, sixteen years his senior, had gone more or less berserk at the death of his beautiful young wife and was of no use in this or anything else, disappearing for long periods of time to return "dirty in person and clothes and penniless," a pattern of behavior that was destined to repeat itself again and again for the rest of his life and cause everybody a good deal of grief including his younger brother.

Jules was therefore the one their father turned to in his troubles, and one way or another he managed to put things back in order. The question then was what was he going to do next. He had no wish to return to the wine business and found no opening in Geneva that appealed to him, so at the age of twenty, without telling anybody what he was about, he made a sudden, dramatic move. Along with eleven other young Genevans, he sailed off to America in order to join the Union army and on May 5, 1862, enlisted as a private under the name of René D'Algers in Company D, 1st Regiment, of the New York Engineer Volunteers, which he told Grammy was made up largely of "roughs and foreigners" and was known as *Les Enfants Perdus*. Each man was supposed to receive a bounty from the state upon enlisting, but he lost his "from falling into the hands of unscrupulous agents," and such was the inauspicious beginning of his career in the country he had come to save.

His motive in coming, he told his wife, was "to help free the slaves," but Uncle Jimmy Kuhn, his grandson, maintained on absolutely no further evidence whatever that the name change clearly meant that he was trying to extricate himself from some romantic entanglement, and Grammy herself seems to refer obliquely to such a possibility. "I do not know that he had any particular reason for wishing to lose himself for a time," she writes, speculating then that "He may have thought that it was more romantic to take a fine sounding name to fight for the freedom of the blacks than to go away with the knowledge of all his friends under his own name which I suppose seemed common to him as he used to say that Golays were as common in Geneva as Smiths are in this country." Who knows? In any case, to America he came, and from then on his "full and busy" years were remarkable for nothing so much as a series of quixotic misadventures that would be the stuff of high comedy if they weren't at the same time so heartbreaking.

The wound he received from the Southern sharpshooter at Petersburg turned out to determine the future course of his life, and Grammy goes into great detail about it both here and when she comes to describing how it resulted finally in his death. The bullet lodged in his right arm a little below the shoulder and landed him in a field hospital where a German who had served in the Crimean War performed the hair-raising surgical procedure known at the time as excision. The five-inch piece of bone that contained the bullet was removed from the upper arm in hopes that the bone at either side would "send out new growth and reunite, causing only a shortening of the limb," but in Jules's case, it didn't work. The upper part of the bone became dead rather than reuniting with the lower, and the arm was held only by skin, flesh, and muscle so that "he could not lift it or stretch it out. When the elbow was supported he could use his hand, but it had to be supported at just the right angle, neither too high nor too low, or he very soon got very tired. When walking he carried his hand usually in his trouser pocket." If anyone jostled him on the street or in a streetcar, the pain was acute. But all of this was to come later.

"For a day or two after the operation he did well," she writes. "Then as there was a prospect of a battle and the Hospital would be needed for the newly wounded, all the patients who were at all able were removed to a Hospital farther away from the field of battle." Jules, however, along with others too sick to move, was left behind untended. Grammy does the best she can to excuse this horror, but you can hear in her voice that it was not easy. "It would seem as if the nurses and doctors must have expected others to have taken their places sooner than they did otherwise they could not have been so heartless and indifferent as to have left those men alone. It was three days that they lay there uncared for, their wounds undressed, in that Southern June. When help at last did come, they were in pitiable condition." But then for the first time since he had arrived in this country, he was lucky, because among those who came was none other than the redoubtable Clara Barton, who with no institutional affiliation or government appointment of any kind but simply out of a sense of duty and a passionate need to heal, brought care to the wounded wherever she found them and eventually became the prime mover in founding the American Red Cross. She stood a slender five feet tall, was twenty-one years older than Jules, and, like the sharpshooter who got him in the shoulder, changed his destiny.

"Jules thought her a veritable angel," Grammy writes, "and she kept her hand on his head while her assistants cleaned the wound. Then followed weary weeks of suffering when it seemed to him he would be in Heaven if only he could lift himself so as to let the cool air under his hot and aching back. Miss Barton had to go to other fields of usefulness but she was attracted to the poor young foreigner so lonely in a strange land and she had managed to talk to him somehow and had

FREDERICK BUECHNER

promised to write." She not only kept her promise, but eventually wrote a long letter also to his father, four or five copies of which are to be found in the grey box together with one in Naya's hand. The style is as orotund and impassioned as a Memorial Day oration, and it is no wonder that it became a family icon. "It is a question in my mind if I shall receive your full forgiveness for the great liberty I take in addressing one to whom I am an entire stranger, a gentleman whose pardon I should have, whose sincerity I should reverence," she begins, but once these politesses are behind her, she launches forth on the high seas. "The son whom you lost, I found. . . . He had come to us on the day of our sorest need and we thanked him; he had struck brave blows for human liberties in a country not his own, and we blessed him; and he had given us forever the manual use of his good right arm, and we loved him." There is a good deal more in this vein, including a description of how she found him "in front of one of our beleaguered cities, fearfully, sadly wounded" and how she feared for his life until "his youth, a strong constitution and a well balanced, vigorous mind, performed wonders for him, and to our surprise he evinced signs of recovery," and then she starts to sound a little less as though she is writing for posterity.

"His assumed relation with myself often brings a smile to my face. While yet he was lying weak and frail in his little army couch, and I had never seen him upon his feet, and never expected to, he asked me one day with all the innocence of a little child if he might be my brother. I replied, 'Yes, my little brother,' for I had never had one and I am greatly his senior.

122

He grasped the promise with all the audacity of a boy and has held it with the firmness of a man. . . . If he sees me sorrowful, he tries to cheer me; if oppressed with care, he tries to help me think; and if he sees my two hands laden, as sometimes must be the case in this singular war life I have led, he comes generously to my side with his one to lighten the burden."

Whether Clara was aware of it or not, the relationship was evidently not without its ambiguities, and Grammy in her forthright, Brewer, Maine, way makes no bones about it. After Jules was sent to a Pennsylvania hospital where he was eventually nursed back to health and discharged from the service, she makes clear that there was no doubt in his mind about what he should do next. "Where would so naturally his feet turn as to Washington where was his only friend," she asks in an odd turn of phrase as though to match the oddness of what she is about to say, "and he became one of the family." And then she comes out and says it. "With a heart full of gratitude for all Miss Barton had done for him, it is not strange that he should have fancied himself in love with her and should have wanted to marry her. She laughed heartily at the notion and showed him his foolishness."

One wonders whether it was Jules himself who told Grammy this or possibly even Miss Barton, whom she must have come to know when she moved to Washington and became Jules's wife. One wonders also about Miss Barton's laughter. In the diary that she kept at about this time she writes a few lines about him that may shed at least a little light. She says she is afraid that she has neglected him too much, what with all her woes and worries, and that he is becoming "habitually unhappy." It had recently turned 1866, and she goes on to add that she has decided to make another New Year's resolution. "I must draw him more tenderly and lovingly to me," she writes, "and *never*," underlining the word, "pain him again if I can help it."

There are two photographs of her occupying places of honor on the front two pages of Jules's album. The first shows her as she must have looked at about the age of forty when he first saw her. She is sitting at a table in profile with her left hand lightly supporting her chin and her right holding open the pages of a book that she seems to be actually reading on the table before her. She has a strong, capable face, but there is great kindness and gentleness in it, beauty even, and you can see how a man young enough to be her son might very well have fallen in love with her. She is faintly smiling. In the second she looks possibly a year or so older, and it shows only her head and the upper part of her shoulders. More than the other, you feel, this is her public face, the one she used in dealing with generals, cabinet ministers, and the heads of governments. It is the one she must have faced her woes and worries with, the one that led Jules to think she was neglecting him. There is a slight air of grimness in her expression, and she looks tired around the eyes as though she has seen too many battlefields, too many young men die.

Some pages farther along in the album is the photograph of a young man who might well have died in the infamous Andersonville prison camp if not on the battlefield, but who survived because his superior penmanship led to his being assigned the task of keeping a roll of the Union soldiers who died during their incarceration. His name was Dorence Atwater, and Grammy has written it above the photograph, which shows a thin-faced young man with a beak of a nose and sideburns well down his jaws. Unknown to his Southern captors, he had made a copy of the fatal roll, and when the war came to an end, he wrote a letter to Miss Barton introducing himself and asking her help in somehow letting the families of those whose names were on it know what had happened to them and how to locate their graves. What Miss Barton decided to do first was advertise in all the leading newspapers of the North that the list was in her possession, "and the letters she received in reply were so numerous," Grammy writes, "that to answer them took all her time and she had to call on Mr. Atwater and Jules to help."

Since Jules had not yet found a job in Washington, it must have pleased him both to have something to do again and also to be able to pay back his benefactress a little for all she had done for him. But unfortunately there was a shadow side to it too. "With all Miss Barton's kind heartedness and desire to help others," Grammy explains, "she was not very constant in her friendship and now Jules who had been her first favorite had to see himself superseded in her affection by Dorence Atwater. Often in approaching the common sitting room he would hear their voices busily engaged in talk but when he entered they had nothing to say to him or each other."

Then the situation became more complicated still. "Miss Barton sent to North Oxford for a niece by marriage, a young lady who had been obliged to give up her work as a singer and teacher of music on account of ill health to come and be the housekeeper." Grammy was wrong about the relationship—the young lady was actually a first cousin once removed, not a niece—but that is more readily understandable than why it was that neither here nor anywhere else in the narrative does she give the young lady's name. She says only that Jules felt keenly what he took to be the loss of Miss Barton's favor "and naturally was led to seek the company of the other exile with the result that after a time they became engaged and later were married and set up their little home in Georgetown where November 13 1867 their daughter Antoinette was born." In other words "a niece by marriage," the "young lady," the "other exile" was Naya's mother and thus my great-grandmother Mattie, or Martha Osgood, Poor.

There is another photograph in Jules's album that I suspect is of her, and I have several reasons, not the least of which is that although Grammy has written in who most of the others were, over this one she has written nothing as though, once again, she could not bring herself, even all those years later, to set down the name of Jules's first love. I have convinced myself too that she resembles Naya a little, especially her oval face and heavily lidded eyes, and that she also doesn't look entirely well. There are shadows under her eyes, and there is something about the slightly slumped way she is sitting and her sad, inward-looking gaze that suggests the invalid. In tiny envelopes, most of them still bearing their original stamps, I have a number of her letters, written in badly faded ink when she was giving piano and singing lessons in Augusta, practicing three hours a day herself, and they are full of a sense of youth and energy that the photograph distinctly lacks. In one of them she describes the boarding house where she was living and writes, "There is an old mission preacher from Mexico here tonight, and he wished to have a sing this evening so to please him we all sang and he sang louder than all the rest of us—he could not sing a tune any more than your Jessie cat can. I had to stand up behind him so that he could not see me laugh." It is hard to picture the young woman with the shadowy, sad eyes laughing.

In any case, rightly or wrongly, I have made up my mind that Mattie Poor is the one in the photograph, and I have a little Minox print I made of it thumbtacked to the window frame over my desk. "The young mother's health continuing to fail," Grammy writes, "in the spring of '68 she and her baby were taken by Jules to Mass. to her Aunt Julie, Mrs. David Barton. He made frequent visits to see her and provided her with every comfort and he had only just left her after one of those visits when he was recalled by her death." Her Aunt Julia, it should be added, was the grandmother of the Edith King who came in her Sunday best to call on us that summer day in Georgetown, Maine, where she found us variously sprawled around the living room like Kentucky moonshiners.

The same year Mattie died, Grammy left Brewer for Washington to take a job at the Treasury Department left vacant by a cousin and made her home with an aunt who took in boarders, including, she says with unusual acerbity, "a superannuated Episcopal clergyman named Withington ... who sat mooning around and was supposed to be engaged in very deep and high thoughts. He was a classmate of Emerson's and had corresponded with him—these facts seemed to set him apart from ordinary mortals and were always mentioned in connection with him." At meals, although he slept elsewhere, there was also a quiet young man with a foreign accent that sometimes made him difficult to understand, who she was told "was a widower and had a little girl in Massachusetts and a good position and was very reliable and of excellent habits." His name, needless to say, was Jules Golay, and the position he held, through the influence of Clara Barton and a senator of her acquaintance, was that of assistant chief of the Bureau of Engraving and Printing at the respectable annual salary of $3500. It was "his work there and what happened there," she says ominously "that determined the whole course of his future life."

It had not happened yet, however, and there under her aunt's roof with Mr. Withington's transcendental gaze upon them, one thing led to another until in time the young pair fell in love and decided to get married. The ceremony took place on December 1, 1869, at Grammy's parents' farm in Brewer "in the front parlor in front of the south window by Mr. Battles the Universalist minister," and soon afterwards they moved into the house in Washington that Jules had found for them right next door to the one occupied by Mr. McCartee, the chief of the Printing Bureau and Jules's boss. "The front room upstairs was our room and was large and sunny and there little Nettie's crib was set up when she came to us in September." She was three years old by then and terribly homesick for her relatives in North Oxford at first, but she soon got over it and came to love Grammy as the only mother she ever really knew.

Somewhere in the grey boxes there is a photograph of the two of them together taken when Grammy must have been in her late eighties. She is all bundled up in a coat and old-lady hat, sitting in a wicker armchair that looks as if it has just been brought out for the purpose on the terrace of the Woodland Road house where she must have been visiting. Her cane is leaning against the shutter of one of the tall French windows behind her. Jamie, about five years old, is standing close to her with his hand on her knee, and I am with Naya, who is wearing a fur piece and has her hand on my shoulder. It must have been about the time I dropped the plush monkey on her head from the top of the stairwell, and only a year or so before she ate such a prodigious amount of corn on her ninetieth birthday.

Her marriage to my great-grandfather had ended with his death about fifty years earlier. It lasted for eleven years and divides into two nearly equal periods—the first spent in Washington, the second in Chicago—both of which were full of disaster. Summing up Jules's life as a whole in the last pages of her account, she speculates as to why this should have been so. "Was he always the victim of wrongdoing or did he himself lack some quality which helped bring about this condition. I cannot help feeling that it was largely the fault of others. . . . Perhaps he lacked the ability to read character and so to see who would help him and who would not, without the painful experience of proving them."

There was one person, however, whose character he came to read all too well, and that was George B. McCartee, his boss. The more he found out about what was going on at the Bureau of Engraving and Printing under McCartee's directorship, the more horrified he became until eventually, Grammy reports, "he and a few others of the employees of the Bureau published anonymously a pamphlet exposing the corrupt way the Bureau was managed, a very foolish and unwise proceeding as Jules realized when it was too late, not but what all they said was true or they thought it was but it was a poor way to bring about their reform." The pamphlet, of which I am sure I have the sole surviving copy, details McCartee's malfeasance and calls for an investigation. Furthermore, it was distributed to all members of Congress and must have made them sit up and take notice with its title page set up in a variety of eye-catching fonts.

STARTLING DISCLOSURES!

THE BUREAU OF ENGRAVING AND PRINTING AND ITS HEAD

A NEST OF CORRUPTION!
A SAINTLY PROFLIGATE !

"WAYS THAT ARE DARK AND TRICKS THAT ARE VAIN!"

AN INVESTIGATION IMPERATIVE

Jules was a lover of Dickens—I remember from Naya's library the collected edition that he had had bound in tawny calf with his name printed on the cover—and my guess is that the Pecksniffian description of McCartee is his.

"He is a professor of religion, a loud professor; a pillar of the church of the Epiphany, one whose voice is heard loudest in the responses, whose Amen is the most sonorous, and whose boots creak the most emphatically when he passes the plate to receive the contributions of the faithful," the pamphlet reads under the heading A SAINTLY DEBAUCHEE, and, elsewhere, "[He is] a man diminutive in stature, and equally in ability and honesty. Within his department he is supreme and irresponsible. He appoints and discharges, he audits and pays, he contracts and purchases, without restraint or supervision. In this nest of corruption . . . he presides over a horde of timid dependents, and is surrounded by an army of spies and informers."

It is stated that there were somewhere between a thousand and fourteen hundred employees of one sort or another at the Bureau—"clerks, bookkeepers, engravers, plate printers," Grammy enumerates them, and among them "a large number of women and girls some of whom counted sheets of paper from the blank sheets to the completed banknotes and stamps of all kinds." Describing them further, she says, "Of course the majority were hardworking women, widows who were by their labor keeping a family of children together, girls who were supporting dependent parents, but . . . there were some girls who were never seen about the Bureau except to sign the pay rolls. It was said they did writing at home." But that was not what everybody said, and whereas Grammy treats the subject with New England reticence, the pamphlet pulls no punches.

"The establishment is an asylum for the paramours of more than one," it charges, "and of those who rank higher than McCartee. [They are] generally distinguished by the small services they perform and the high wages they receive; and this to the disgust of the honest who are compelled to live in association with those who subsist on what they consider the wages of prostitution." What is more, it continues, "Several months ago the widow of the lately deceased chief clerk of the Bureau was discovered by the lady in whose house she lodged in the act of having illicit intercourse with Geo. B. McCartee." Nor was sexual misconduct all that the document charges him with. He was guilty, it says, of gross mismanagement, nepotism, bribe-taking, extorting money from the Treasury Department by charging it high for the cheapest kind of ink, paper, and the like in order to pocket the difference, and in general bilking the government for all it was worth.

Jules's motives were, as always, of the noblest. As a man of honor and a loyal American citizen, he felt he could do no less than tell the truth as he knew it and was confident that once it was told, the government would throw the rascal out. What happened, of course, was that he was in effect thrown out himself. Suspecting that he was the one behind the exposé, wicked little Mr. McCartee, his one-time neighbor and friend, made things so increasingly uncomfortable for him at the Bureau that it was not long before he felt obliged to tender his resignation, thus losing the only decent salary he ever earned.

Luckily, however, having for some time suspected that his days at the Bureau were numbered, he had already started a small jewelry business across the street from the Treasury building with the idea that his father back in Geneva would keep him stocked with the watches and other things that he would offer for sale there. Not wanting Mr. McCartee, for whom he was still working, to get wind that he was contemplating departure, he looked around for someone to be the ostensible manager, and this time it was Grammy herself who proved to be a poor judge of character because she recommended "a favorite cousin of my girlhood" named Clinton Morrill, who had served as Jules's best man when they were married in Brewer. The picture of him on the next to last page of the album shows a rather handsome if somewhat weak-looking young man with a soup-strainer moustache, a cleft chin, and eyes that seem to be slightly out of focus.

"It was a most unfortunate suggestion on my part tho' made ignorantly and innocently," she writes, and then goes on to explain that "Clinton's weakness was unknown to me tho' as I afterward found out well known to everybody else in Bangor," which was where at the time he was working as a clerk in Mr. Brown's corn and flour store. Clinton's weakness was that he was a hopeless alcoholic. "He rarely drank enough to be unfitted to wait on customers after a fashion but he was talkative and laughed in a silly way and women and girls began to dislike to come into the store." To make matters worse, the Swiss repairman they hired, named Robert, was not much better. "[He] began to be careless, did not come promptly as at first, sometimes did not come at all and when he did come was not fit to do his work properly."

As if all this was not enough, Jules's father took to occasionally letting his older son, Abraham, be the one to ship goods to Washington for his brother to sell, and the results were as might have been expected. On one occasion Abraham dispatched a great number of expensive music boxes that Jules had not ordered, "and they were put on every available chair and table even on the floor in our parlor for there was no room for so many in the store," and although eventually Jules managed to dispose of them all, he took a financial loss doing so. As Grammy puts it, "a business that had three such men as Robert, Clinton, and Abraham connected with it was pretty heavily handicapped and Jules had with reason many anxious hours." But the worst was still to come.

Having by now left the Bureau for good, Jules came out in the open about the jewelry store's being his and substituted his name for Clinton's on the sign out front. Not unpredictably, it didn't take long for his former boss to make his move. As Grammy says, "[Jules] might have made a success of the business if Mr. McCartee had not used his powerful influence with his employees among whom were Jules's greatest number of acquaintances to keep them away from the store," and of course the sales plummeted. By this time he had become the father of two other daughters, had been enormously generous to his Brewer in-laws and various Swiss compatriots who came to him for help, and he finally made the decision that he had better close the business down once and for all while he still had some money left and seek his fortune elsewhere.

There are two pictures in the album of a woman named Carrie Morrill Brown, who was the wayward Clinton's mother. One of them shows her looking pensive and forlorn in widow's weeds of great elegance—a wide black bow under her chin, a veil, a magnificent black dress with pleats and shirring—and in the other one she is holding a baby son in her lap. In this one, as in the earlier, she is far more fashionably gotten up than any other woman in the album; her velvet dress has a lace collar and embroidered cuffs, her hair is beautifully coifed with three curls hanging loosely down to one shoulder, and she is wearing earrings. Grammy does not tell her story, but from what she says incidentally here and there it would seem that after the death of Clinton's father, Carrie was married again to a rich man from Chicago named Brown and, at the time Jules was having his hard times in Washington, was for some reason living in Europe with a fräulein to help with the two babies from her second marriage.

To summarize a story that Grammy tells in considerable detail, Carrie came back from Europe, learned about her son's "dissipated habits," and, because she believed that Jules exerted a good influence on the young man, "strongly urged him to go with her to Chicago where she felt sure that through the business acquaintances of her husband and herself she could help Jules and Clinton into business ... and would make every effort to keep them together." You hardly know whether to laugh or to cry. With nothing better in sight, Jules allowed himself to be persuaded, moved his family west, and thus began the final chapter of his life.

The business that Carrie bought for her son and his friend had to do with the selling of something called Comet Fire

Kindlers, "which were made," Grammy explains "by filling a cone of stout brown paper with first bits of soft coal and then larger pieces the whole covered with coal tar to be placed in the stove in front of the draft and then covered with the ordinary coal." It apparently worked well, and so at first did the business, with Jules managing the store and keeping the accounts while Clinton went out on the road making sales and deliveries. But then, as might have been predicted, "Clinton fell back into his old habits of drinking," and the old story began all over again. "The wagon loaded with kindlers ... would stand for hours in front of some one of the beer saloons of which Chicago was full while Clinton drank his beer, played cards, talked or dozed in a chair," and things went from bad to worse until finally Jules advised Carrie to stop putting her money in it, and she eventually sold out at a considerable loss.

Two good things happened in Chicago, however. One of them was that in the summer of 1878 "Jules was called back to Washington as a witness in the investigation of the affairs of the Printing Bureau during which all and more than he had ever charged Mr. McCartee with was proved and he was dismissed." The other was that after a long, dispiriting search for any work he could find, made all the more difficult by the increasing pain of his useless right arm, he finally landed a job as bookkeeper in a hardware store at $60 a month—a far cry from the $3500 a year he had earned at the Bureau, but more than anything he had managed since—and the family moved out of Carrie Brown's house into an apartment "up two flights over a beer saloon with the sign of the wife of the proprietor as midwife decorating the front entrance." But no matter. "It was on a car line near enough to the children's school and not too far for Jules to walk down town in good weather.... The children were given a cat and a dog.... Antoinette had a canary, later Cornelia had one too and Juliette had a gold fish" with the result that all in all, as Grammy sums it up, "I look back upon the time we lived in those five rooms as almost the happiest time of my life."

Not even the unheralded arrival of Abraham in the winter of 1879 spoiled things. He had met Clara Barton when she stayed with the senior Golays on one of her visits to Geneva, and his American relatives knew that he had come from Switzerland in steerage to visit her while she was taking the water cure for nervous and physical exhaustion in Dansville, New York. What effect his presence had on her condition can only be guessed, but in any event Jules was quick to write urging him not to make the journey to Chicago to see them because he would never find work there. Work, however, not being Abraham's long suit, he came anyway, and Grammy and Jules laughed "over the amazement of the other clerks in the store at the strange appearance of the foreign-looking man dressed in the cheapest kind of ready made suit with long straggling iron grey hair and beard and not too clean who rushed up to Jules and kissed him on both cheeks talking volubly excited French all the time."

That summer, on Thursday, July 8, 1880, at the age of thirty-eight, Jules died in the Alexian Hospital of blood poisoning that set in after the emergency amputation of his right arm, which was brought about by abscessing and unbearable pain. Grammy devotes the final twenty pages of her hundred-odd-page narrative to his last days, and I remember Naya telling me once that while they were going on—she was twelve years old—one of her friends told her that if she wore a dime in her shoe, her father would get better.

He was buried in Graceland Cemetery with Grammy and the children of course in attendance together with Abraham and a handful of others, and when I was teaching at Wheaton College just about a hundred years later, I went there once to see if I could find the spot among all those towering old trees and stretches of shadowy grass. My English Department colleague Roger Lundin and his wife, Sue, took me there, but although we all of us looked for a long time we were never able to find it. It was only when I read back over Grammy's description that I found that at his own request, not wanting his family to incur any unnecessary expenses, he was buried in an unmarked grave.

On that same bottom shelf near the fireplace where Grammy's account is, there is another book that has to do with Jules Golay. It also is in a box that Posy and I made for it and contains a story he wrote out by hand in his lovely, lucid French to give Naya for Christmas 1878. It is called *La Fée aux Roses* and is a graceful little tale about a mother and father bird and their three babies who live in the topmost branches of a very tall pine tree that grows in the Jura near a waterfall. Led on by a wicked fairy named Envy, sinister black animals gnaw away at the tree's roots until it is so weakened that when a fierce storm comes up, it goes crashing, and the whole family is killed in the fall. When the Rose Fairy herself, whose name is Friendship, buries them among the moss and lichen that grow at the bottom of a glacier, from their tomb spring beautiful red rhododendrons and blue gentians that eventually spread all through the Alps, but otherwise it is a fairy tale without a happy ending.

seven

In addition to the autographed photograph of Anthony Trollope that hangs in the library near Queen Elizabeth's abandoned signature, there is a framed *Spy* caricature of him in the hallway that runs from the family archives to the office. His bushy whiskers have turned white, and his fierce, ruddy face bears out Henry James's "all gobble and glare." He is wearing baggy grey trousers and a black frock coat that strains over his pot belly to reveal a silver watch chain looped through his waistcoat. He is standing up, bald and bespectacled, facing directly forward with his left hand behind his back and his left knee slightly bent. In his right hand he is holding a smoking cigar between his index and middle fingers, his thumb upraised, and seems to be gesturing with it as he presses some point home. "Trollope would bluster and rave and roar, blowing and blustering like a grampus," his Post Office colleague Edmund Yates wrote, "scarcely giving himself time to think, but roaring out an instantly-formed opinion couched in the very strongest terms." Over his left shoulder, there is a puff of smoke as if he has just swept his cigar vigorously through the air to demolish some fool he is not suffering gladly. Nothing could be more foolish than the text that accompanies the caricature. "He is a student and delineator of costume rather than of humanity," it says. "He is a correct painter of the small things of our small modern English life so far as it presents itself to the eye—deeper than that he does not go."

Trollope is, of course, one of the immortals. Over the years I have read at least twenty of his forty-eight novels out loud to my wife on long drives, and of the others I have read by myself all but two or three obscure ones like *Linda Tressel* and *Nina Balatka*, which I am saving for a rainy day. Once we got hopelessly lost in Boston traffic because we were so spellbound by the great scene in which Ferdinand Lopez throws himself under a railway train at Tenby Junction in *The Prime Minister* that we lost all sense of where we were or where we were going. Tolstoy, who was reading it at the time he was writing *Anna Karenina*, may well have conceived Anna's death under its influence, and it was Tolstoy too who wrote, "Trollope kills me, kills me, with his excellence."

Some fifteen years ago or so I read *The Last Chronicle of Barset* aloud in bits and pieces as we made the fifteen-hundred-mile drive from Vermont to Florida with one dachshund or another dozing on top of the luggage piled in the back seat, and now we are reading it again because it seems to me that possibly, as Trollope himself believed, it is his best. Let all take a good look at it who go to him for nothing more than that coziness, and Englishness, and sunlit mid-Victorian tranquillity that led to his becoming "the great national bomb shelter" of World War II. *The Last Chronicle* is positively Dostoyevskian in its exploration of the labyrinthine depths of the human spirit as they exist in the tormented figure of Josiah Crawley, perpetual curate of Hogglestock, that bitter, broken, self-pitying, self-flagellating, and above all else proudful man whom there is good reason to believe Trollope based at least in part on his half-mad failure of a father. He is among the most pitiable as well as the most exasperating of Trollope's vast number of characters, and yet it is he who in the end dares enter into mortal combat with the great comic villain Mrs. Proudie, the Bishop's unspeakable wife. "On her shoulders she wore a short cloak of velvet and fur, very handsome withal, but so swelling in its proportions on all sides as necessarily to create more of dismay than of admiration in the mind of any ordinary man. And her bonnet was a monstrous helmet with the beaver up, displaying the awful face of a warrior, always ready for combat, and careless to guard itself from attack. The large, contorted bows which she bore were as a grisly crest upon her casque, beautiful, doubtless, but majestic and fear-compelling. In her hand she carried her armour all complete, a prayer-book, a Bible, and a book of hymns."

"No one ever on seeing Mr. Crawley took him to be a happy man, or a weak man, or an ignorant man, or a wise man," Trollope writes, and with his shaggy brows and furrowed cheeks he faces down the old dragon before the aghast and admiring

eyes of her husband and so thoroughly trounces her that the
wounds prove fatal. Then all at once Trollope reveals—having
heretofore only hinted at it, perhaps only partly seen it himself—how she is in her own way as complex and pitiable as
Crawley: a good woman gone appallingly wrong, a disgrace to
her husband in her effort to be his strong right arm, and so
tyrannical in her Christian zeal "that not a soul in the world
loved her, or would endure her presence if it could be avoided."
Most pitiable of all, she knows it, and, following her utter defeat
by Mr. Crawley and with the silence with which the Bishop
answers her "I suppose then that you wish I were dead?" still
ringing in her ears, she goes up to her room and locks the door.
It is her maid who comes upon her soon afterwards, dead of an
apoplectic stroke. "The body was still resting on its legs, leaning
against the end of the side of the bed, while one of the arms was
close clasped round the bed-post. The mouth was rigidly close,
but the eyes were as though staring . . ."

It is the sound of Trollope's voice that I think I cherish most
about him. He never rants or preaches or sobs like Dickens. He
is rarely ironic or arch like Jane Austen, or tongue-in-cheek like
Thackeray, whom he knew and much admired. He simply goes
on speaking unostentatiously, clearly, honestly, as if there is all
the time in the world for telling us everything he wants us to
know in order to spin out his tale. He must have saved all his
bombast and bad manners for the Garrick Club or the fox hunt,
because the man the books reveal is decent, humane, and
uncommonly sensitive to the workings of the human heart, particularly the hearts of young women, who, unlike their either

saccharine or grotesque counterparts in Dickens, are among his subtlest and most convincing creations. Nothing is too small to escape his notice, including the two tears that trickle down Archdeacon Grantly's nose when that most worldly and over-bearing man is so taken with Josiah Crawley's daughter Grace that he tells her that if her father is ever cleared of the criminal charges against him, he will forget all his previous objections and accept her as the wife of his son after all.

In his autobiography he is mostly concerned with his professional life—which books he wrote when, how many copies each sold, how they were received by the reviewers, and so on—but there is one place where he reveals something that seems close to the secret of who he was. "I have long been aware," he writes, "of a certain weakness in my own character, which I may call a craving for love. I have ever had a wish to be liked by those around me—a wish that during the first half of my life was never gratified." It is because he saw it as a weakness, of course, that he gobbled and glared and snorted so that no one would ever guess, but it is there in his books for all the world to see. He wanted people to like not only him, but those bits and pieces of him who were his characters. He wanted them to forgive Mrs. Proudie for being a bully, and Josiah Crawley for being a hopeless neurotic, and Obadiah Slope for being Obadiah Slope, as he himself forgave them and hoped he himself would be forgiven.

This is why, with few if any exceptions beyond the infamous Barry Lynch in his second novel, *The Kellys and the O'Kellys*, he was incapable of creating real villains. He knew too much about what made them who they were, understood too well that we are all of us flawed. There is no greater scoundrel anywhere in his fiction than the rapacious swindler Augustus Melmotte in *The Way We Live Now*, but even as his crimes begin to catch up with him and he realizes that the world is crumbling about his ears when the great dinner he gives at the government's request for the emperor of China proves more or less of a failure, he steps out into the night and pauses for a moment, looking up at the bright stars.

"If he could be there, in one of those unknown, distant worlds, with all his present intellect and none of his present burdens, he would, he thought, do better than he had done here on earth. If he could even now put himself down nameless, fameless, and without possessions in some distant corner of the world, he could, he thought, do better. But he was Augustus Melmotte, and he must bear his burdens, whatever they were, to the end. He could reach no place so distant but that he would be known and traced." Melmotte was a black scoundrel, but Trollope can't leave it at that. He wants us to understand that he was also a human being.

Along with his bold signature, Trollope has written "Very faithfully" on a little card beneath the photograph of him that hangs in the library, and so faithful were the likenesses he drew that I need him now to help me draw one of my brother, Jamie, who died as I was writing these last few pages. He was two and a half years younger than I am and would have been seventy on his next birthday. We were the only two children in our family. I can't imagine the world without him. I can't imagine him without the world.

I want to get him right the way Trollope would have gotten him right. I want especially to get his way of laughing right. I want to get it right about how on his visits to see us in Vermont when everybody else was dithering around trying to decide what to do next, he would sit out on the lawn in his sweater and khaki pants reading the *Times* in utter peace as he puffed on one of the appalling little cigars he wasn't allowed to smoke inside. I want to get it right about the way he took life as it came instead of, like me, brooding about the past or worrying himself sick about the future.

I also want to get it right about whatever it is that is going on inside me now. There is the level of feeling where, after moments when the clouds seem to be lifting a little, it is suddenly all I can do to see the hand in front of my face. And there is the level of thinking, thinking back especially over our last few conversations, including the one within only three or four hours of his death when we said good-bye for good. But deeper down still there is a level that I know nothing about at all except that whatever I am doing there, it is absolutely exhausting. It is as if great quantities of furniture have to be moved from one place to another. There seem to be endless cartons of God only knows what to sort through somehow. The earth itself has to be bulldozed and shifted around and reshaped. A whole new landscape has to come into being.

As legend has it, I was taken to see him for the first time at Miss Lippincott's, a New York lying-in hospital where it was fashionable to be born at this period, when he was only a day or so old. According to my mother, he was a scrawny little thing, and to make up for it she was eager for the nurses and doctors to see her cherubic firstborn as well. My father was the one who brought me, and, according again to my mother, I put on a horrifying act as he led me to her room, walking all doubled over with my eyes rolling around in my head and my jaw hanging loose. But apparently things looked up as soon as I saw the baby. I said I wanted to recite him something, and I did. What I chose was, "One misty moisty morning when cloudy was the weather, I chanced to meet an old man all dressed up in leather," and it marked the beginning of a relationship that lasted for just short of seventy years.

For the first seven or eight of them, I'm afraid that in the way of big brothers I made his life miserable. At that point the two and a half years' difference in our ages seemed to put us in different generations, and I must have felt that it was bad enough simply to have a rival at all, let alone one whose youth and lack of experience were a continual source of embarrassment to me. When we lived in Washington in 1932 I was sent off to first grade at a school run by two French spinsters known as the Misses Maret, where all classes were conducted in the French language including music, which we were taught by an old lady who played the piano in spite of being blind as a bat so that we spent most of the time making terrible faces at her with no fear of reprisal. Apparently I let my brother walk part of the way to school with me, but always made him turn back well before we got there so nobody would discover my shame.

I have that detail only on my mother's word, but I actually remember one summer in Quogue, Long Island, sticking a wad of bubble gum in his hair so that when Energine failed to get rid of it, it had to be cut out with scissors leaving a disfiguring patch of bald scalp, and on another occasion throwing a fat green caterpillar at him which sent him into hysterics when it burst to pieces on his shirt. Sometimes I would simply look at him and gibber nonsense syllables until he could take it no longer and started to scream. For fear the racket would bring our parents' wrath down upon me, I developed a sure-fire technique for stopping him. If only he would be quiet, I said, I would give him my *Uncle Wiggily* books, and it always worked like a charm. Most of them have my name in them, Frebby, but you can see where in one or two he managed to add his too, using an electrically heated stylus we had that you could write with through strips of variously colored gold, silver, and bronze metallic paper. Probably because he knew the transaction would never hold up in court, he always seemed to take it for granted that in time the books reverted automatically to me, and thus the bribe worked for years. I also told him that he was a foundling someone had left on our doorstep in a basket and that when he walked, his corduroy knickerbockers squeaked in a ridiculous way and that his garters showed. This was roughly at the time when, at the arrival of some visitors in our house, we could hear him muttering something over and over again under his breath, and when we asked him later what it had been, he said it was the number six, six, six, six, because he knew they would probably ask him how old he was and he wanted to be ready with the answer. Every once in a while when we were in our fifties or so he would suddenly turn on me and cry out, "You ruined my childhood!" to which I would answer that he was ruining my old age, and then, together, we would rock with seismic laughter.

I suppose it was by a gradual process that we changed from victim and victimizer to best friends, but a major step along the way must have come soon after dawn on Saturday, November 21, 1936, when Jamie was a month short of eight and I only a few months past ten. Staying in our room as we had been told, we looked down from what seemed a dizzying height to where our mother and grandmother in their nightdresses had managed to drag the young man who was our father from the garage out onto the driveway and, with no idea in the world how to do it, were trying to revive him. I picture us up there as we would have appeared from below. We are framed by the window in our pajamas, and in different ways for each of us I suspect that we remained there, side by side, always.

What happened next was that, confirming all her Buechner in-laws' view of her as extravagant, irresponsible, and hopelessly spoiled, my mother decided that, although she had never been there, the place we should go in order to start a new life was, of all places, Bermuda, and it was there that I stopped persecuting my brother once and for all and our friendship blossomed. It was there too, I think, that for the first time I began to see our lives in both chronological and more or less logical sequence, as a part of real history, whereas before there seemed only chaos as we moved from place to place so often that every year there was a different house, a different school, a different woman to take care of us, and the only common thread was the fights between our parents that continually threatened to blow the whole show to bits.

Like most Bermuda houses, ours had a name, the Moorings, and was situated in Paget right on the harbor directly across from Hamilton, so that we could fish for things like squirrel fish and sergeant majors off the terrace, always throwing them back because they were too small and too beautiful to do anything else with, and fly kites over the water without getting them tangled in trees. We also had a rowboat, more Jamie's cup of tea than mine, and I can picture him at the oars, a small, wiry figure, with his white visored cap on backwards and his eyes squinnied against the sun. To go to Hamilton, we took a ferry called *The Dragon*, whose stern rode perilously low in the water and which I always thought looked like a foreign legionnaire's hat when they rolled canvas down along the sides and back to shield the passengers in bad weather, the foredeck piled high with bikes, which in those pre–World War II days were the only means of transportation there was unless you could afford a horse and carriage or took the little narrow-gauge railway that ran down the center of the island. More than Jamie, who like our father was an outdoor person, a rowboat person, I was dazzled by the Hamilton shops. There was Guerlain's down by the ferry dock, fragrant with L'Heure Bleue, our mother's favorite; and the Golden Gate, where you could buy everything from mangoes and papaws to beach toys, cedarwood letter openers, glass paperweights with real butterflies inside them, and ladies' underwear; the Goodie Shoppe, which downstairs had Peak Frean biscuits in tins with the new King and Queen emblazoned on the lids, not to mention Cadbury chocolates of every possible description; and upstairs a tearoom where once in a while for a treat we went for charlottes russes. There were also the Indian shops, which sold filmy, tie-dyed scarves and silver filigree jewelry, and the Bermuda Bookstore, which smelled the way only a new book from England does when you open it for the first time, faintly like nutmeg, dry, erudite. Trimingham's was the most elegant of them all in those days— Irish tweeds, cashmere sweaters and jackets, camel's-hair polo coats, English luggage that gleamed like old saddles—and in the ladies' department there was a clerk named Mrs. Bunting, with soft blonde hair and blue eyes who always called Jamie "Lover" so that he hid whenever he saw her coming.

There was nothing like the number of tourists back then that there came to be later when they could make the trip by air in no time flat instead of taking one or the other of the two top-heavy Cunarders, the *Monarch* and the *Queen of Bermuda*, that made the regular run from New York. It was still a foreign country in those days with a different way of speaking, a different kind of money and weather, a different form of government with a royal governor who on state occasions such as the coronation of George VI wore a cocked hat with white plumes on it like the captain of the *Pinafore*. Almost most striking of all, there were no motor vehicles of any kind, just the clip-clop of horses and the silvery carillon of carriage bells and bicycle bells.

At the school we went to, Warwick Academy, Jamie and I were the only Americans as far as I can remember and for that reason attracted a good deal of unwanted attention. Nobody had ever called us Yankees before, and I remember my horror at being asked which I liked better, President Roosevelt or the King, because I was afraid that if I said the King I would be guilty of treason and if I said the President I might be thrown off the island. The headmaster, Major Welsh, was a small Scotsman who looked like Savonarola and used the term "bickety-bock" to refer to the instrument he used for paddling you with if you forgot your homework or cut up in class, and my classroom master was Mr. Sutton, a large, florid Englishman with china teeth and a habit of lighting his Player cigarettes with the sun through a magnifying glass that he kept in his blazer pocket. On one occasion, before my unbelieving eyes, he tied string around the thumbs of a boy whose defiant face I can still remember, threw it over the top of the door, and then pulled down on it with such strength that the boy was literally dancing on his toes on the other side. As Americans, Jamie and I seemed to be exempt from such measures, but you could never be sure what might happen next, and it gave us food for thought. Like the shadow of the past, it was another part, I suspect, of what drew us closer together than we had ever been before.

As nearly as it is possible to reenter my self in those days, it seems to me that I had somehow managed to put that shadow so far behind me or deep within me that it was as if it had never been at all. We lived surrounded by fields of Easter lilies and Bermuda onions, by white coral roads that dried in minutes after even the most torrential rain, by pink coral beaches that we biked to after school to swim in Gulf Stream waters that went from aquamarine to turquoise to celery green as they neared the shore. The air was fragrant with the dwarf cedars that grew everywhere in those days, before they were killed by the blight, and the complex scent of horses, kerosene stoves, and the salt sea air. In the midst of all that, for me, everything that had come earlier vanished without a trace. But not so for Jamie.

I came upon him once all by himself in his bedroom crying and when I asked him why, he wouldn't tell me. Was it this? Was it that? But all he would finally say was that it was something that had happened a long time ago—a year is a long time when you've lived so few of them—and only then did I realize with a jolt that he was of course crying about our father. I would never have known of it except by accident, he would never have told me if I hadn't dragged it out of him, and all his life he remained such a profoundly private person that when I wrote a fictionalized version of our childhood called *The Wizard's Tide*, for his sake I changed him into a little girl. He kept his feelings almost entirely to himself, didn't like "direct questions" as he put it, and I remember my delight in overhearing the way he handled one once at a cocktail party in Florida. A very energetic, cause-oriented woman asked him what he did with his life now that he had retired, and what he said to her was that the first thing he did every morning was count the sections of his breakfast grapefruit and that she might be interested to know the number was by no means always the same.

Needless to say, the feelings remained deep down inside him, although not because he had unconsciously repressed them there, I think, but simply because deep down was where, like a furnace in the cellar, he felt they belonged. Only on the rarest occasions did they ever surface. Once when he was leafing through *Listening to Your Life*, a collection of quotations from my books for every day of the year, I asked him to look up and read me the one for his birthday, December 7. It turned out to be a passage about how when our mother was in her nineties, she asked me one day who the man was that had just passed by her window and, when I told her it was the gardener, said, "Tell him to come in and take a look at the last rose of summer." Suddenly, he stopped in the middle of a sentence and I could see that he could read no farther. Another time was when he went with us once to what turned out to be an extraordinarily moving Blanche Moyse performance of the *St. Matthew Passion* in Marlboro, Vermont, and after it was over, when I asked him what he had thought of it, he was literally unable to speak.

He wrote a poem or two in the guest book we tried to keep for a while. "Japanese candy tastes like punk. / That's the word for today from Uncle Skunk" one of them goes, and another, perhaps even more eloquent, "I tied a daisy to a rock. / When I threw it into Beebe Pond, it went plock."

He also collected malapropisms he enjoyed using from time to time like "eyebulb," "red leather day," and "You might as well be hung for a sheep as a groat," and when he retired from the bank where for years he worked without much enthusiasm as a public-relations officer, he took to puttering around with electronics in their apartment in a nineteenth-century Madison Avenue brownstone, where he and his wife, Jackie, lived for all the years of their marriage. It was my mother who rented it first in 1946, so the way Jamie reckoned it, it has been in the family for something like half of its existence. When my mother married for the third time and moved out of it down to North Carolina, I lived there alone for a time trying to write one early novel or another. Sunday after Sunday I would go to the church next door to hear George Buttrick preach sermons that ended up changing my life and eventually started off from there to attend Union Theological Seminary for the first time, making the trip on the Number-Four Fifth Avenue bus, which went up as far as the Cloisters and Fort Tryon Park as for all I know it still does. In 1954 when Jamie got out of the army, where he ended up as a second lieutenant at Fort Sill, Oklahoma, he and I lived there together for a time. It was during this period that we drove south to visit our mother, who decided to use our presence as an excuse for throwing a large cocktail party "to meet James and Frederick Buechner" as the invitation read, which made it sound, we decided, as though she was announcing our engagement.

The apartment that, with his wife, Jamie lived in all those years and finally died in is on the third floor, up a flight of fifty-two sagging, dimly lit steps, and in a small room off the living room he worked at a table turning out strange flickering, beeping electronic devices which he housed in the little wooden boxes that dried codfish comes in. Two of the ones he made for me still work. One of them is a cross that blinks, first the horizontal beam marked OPEN, and then the vertical one marked HEART, which comes down through the E with a small red heart at the end of OPEN to balance things out the way I described it in the second of the Bebb books; and the other is a delicate, matchstick rendition of the Emerald City with three turrets, each bearing a green pennant marked OZ, that at the push of a button tinkles out a tiny, electronic version of "Over the Rainbow." He made a good many of them over the years for various friends and relations, several of them boxes that would answer any question you put to them with YES, NO, or MAYBE. When he was trying to decide what to call them, I suggested *ignis fatuus*, which he liked though neither of us ever got around to figuring out what the plural would be.

Our father's death never seemed to haunt him the way for more than sixty years it has haunted me, partly, I think, because he laid it to rest by grieving over it, whereas both my mother and I carried on as though the man had never even lived, let alone died. Partly, too, I think it was because he was just enough younger than I not to have been so affected by all the sadness and disorder that surrounded it, although there was one period, during which we were staying at Naya's house on Woodland Road while our father was off looking for yet another job, when under the pretext that his clothes didn't fit right he refused more or less for an entire winter to get up and dressed in the mornings because, I can only guess, bed was the safest, sanest, most comforting place he knew. But mainly, I suspect, it was simply not in his nature to dwell on the past any more than it was to agonize about the future. Even during the last year of his life this was so. He was subjected to all sorts of painful medical and surgical procedures that I would have ruined weeks of my life dreading, whereas he took them as completely in his stride as trips to the dentist. When he finally learned that there was nothing more the doctors could do for him except try to control the increasing pain, I disregarded his distaste for direct questions and asked him how he felt about it. His answer was simply that he looked forward to its all being over soon more than he had ever looked forward to anything in his life.

The last time we met was a month or so before the fatal diagnosis was made. I had to speak at Trinity Church on Wall Street and made a detour on my way from Penn Station to see him. It was a brief, hectic visit, most of which I spent trying to find out with the help of a map he produced where on earth in the bowels of Manhattan my hotel was and how I was going to get there. He had lost a fair amount of weight by then and a good deal of energy, but he looked well, his color was good, and he seemed to have no doubt that everything was going to be all right. Though the fifty-two steps were something of a challenge, he said, he made himself go out every day, and when it came time for me to leave, he said he would leave with me. It was a sunny, windy spring day on Madison Avenue, and we spoke about how he and Jackie would be coming up for my birthday in a few weeks. Then a taxi appeared so suddenly that I barely had time to shake his hand before I was off on my way, not dreaming that we would never shake hands again.

What did he look like? Trollope sometimes tells you so much—describing in turn the hair, brow, eyes, lips, teeth, nose—that you end up seeing everything except the face they all add up to. He was on the short side, well built, a little thick around the middle in his later years but with his wife's constant vigilance always managing to trim down before it got out of hand. When he was young, people thought he looked like the young Bobby Kennedy. When he was older, he told our mother one day that when he was standing in front of the bathroom mirror before he had shaved his stubble that morning, he decided he was a dead ringer for Yasir Arafat, to which her reply was that he should be so lucky. Maybe what people remember most vividly about him is his laugh—not just the way he did it, with his head thrown back, putting all he had into it, all he *was* into it, holding back nothing—but the way you could see him getting ready to do it, waiting for you to set it off by doing something or saying something funnier than anything you could possibly have managed without him. My laughter when it gets out of control becomes a series of falsetto hoots that embarrass me because they don't sound at all like who I think I am, but his was totally who he was, the richest and the best of himself that he had to give. We had only to think of something along the lines of his theatrical debut as Alice with long golden curls in a Trinity School production of the Mad Tea Party—Jamie was in the third grade, I was in the sixth, and a little oddball named Truman Capote was in the seventh—and we would fall to pieces. Or to remember something like our mother's remark, a propos of his ultraconservative taste in clothes, that whenever she went looking for a necktie to give him for his birthday, she always told the clerk that she was buying it for her grandfather.

He had hazel eyes and strong, white teeth, and his feet sometimes tended to turn out a little when he walked. He had a good head of hair and never wore hats except a knitted wool one pulled down to his eyebrows when he came up to see us winters. When we went walking in the snow, he often carried an ash staff about as tall as he was which one or the other of our daughters had cut and decorated for him. Into the bark she carved a heart, a cross like the one on the Swiss flag surrounded by a shield, and his initials, J.K.B. Underneath, spiraling downwards, is the word *salzstengel,* which for reasons long forgotten was some kind of a family joke, and beneath it *Mum Mum,* which was what he was apt to say when he was about to dig into, or "fang" as he sometimes put it, some dish that he was especially fond of. At the bottom it says Christmas 1978. It leans now against the back wall of the guest-room closet where he last left it.

He was an unassuming man—he assumed nothing about the people he met, plain or fancy, except that the chances were he would find something about them that was either interesting or entertaining. And an unpretentious man—he made no pretense at being anything he wasn't, but seemed to accept himself for better or worse the way he accepted pretty much everybody else. For years he was a shy, rather quiet man until you got to know him, but over the years his gregarious, supportive wife, whom he loved, brought him out a good deal. For reasons known only to them, they never had any children, but if it bothered him, he never said so. As far as I know, he never bore a grudge, and I can't remember ever hearing him speak a cruel word or a deceitful one. I have never known anybody braver. As an old friend wrote in a sentence that sounds a little like the great Anthony himself, "He was always for me one of the loveliest men I had ever come to know."

It was on July 11, 1998 the day I turned seventy-two, that he phoned me to say that he had been told he had incurable cancer of virtually everything and didn't intend to be around for more than two weeks more if he could possibly help it. He then added, "By the way, Happy Birthday," at which he managed somehow to give his extraordinary laugh once again, with some fractured, hopeless echo of it from me. "I've told Jackie to think of it not as losing a husband but as gaining half a closet." I told him that I would come down right away to New York to see him, but though he never in so many words asked me not to—there wasn't much to see was what he said—I knew that was the way he wanted it. And it was the way I wanted it too. The alternative, we came to agree, was too harrowing to think about. Instead, we talked almost every day on the telephone, and that way we could go on believing that there would always be another time still and another time after that, whereas a last visit would be the last and we both would know it.

When I called him on the afternoon of Saturday, July 25, I said, remembering about his two-week deadline, that it must be that the end wasn't very far off. He said that it had already started and that it was the happiest day of his life. Although he was a dying man, he in no way either sounded or seemed like a sick man. He said how good it had been to see Judy earlier in the day. She had gone down to be with Jackie, and I decided I had to go with her despite the earlier agreement, but was saved by a cold and fever. I told him that I had loved him as much as I had ever loved anybody in my life, and forgetting about the green caterpillar and the bubble gum, he said, "You have been a wonderful brother." I said I had a feeling we had not seen the last of each other, and he made a soft, descending "Ah-h-h" sound as a way to thank me for saying it, for maybe even believing it. Then I said I guessed this was good-bye, and he said yes, and then we both started to cry so that there was nothing more we could do but hang up, he in the old brownstone on Madison Avenue and I in what our grandson Dylan calls "the breakable room," rarely used because it is filled with things too precious to risk breaking and now with this other precious thing.

One of our sons-in-law, David, was with him when he died a few hours later, and Jamie told him how he wished he knew how to thank him properly for all he had done, flying down from Boston four or five times those last few days to help him wind things up in every conceivable way. He said he wished he had some way to repay him for his inconceivable kindness, to which David replied that I had once said I might think about giving him the Uncle Wiggily books. "If I were you, I'd try to get that in writing," Jamie said, and those were among the last of all his words.

He never went to church except once in a while to hear me, and he didn't want a funeral, he told me—too much like a direct question, I suppose—but when I suggested maybe cocktails and dinner for some of his old friends in the fall when everybody got back to the city, he said that sounded like a good idea. But he did ask me if I would write a prayer for him that he could use, and David said that he had it there on the table beside him.

"Dear Lord, bring me through darkness into light. Bring me through pain into peace. Bring me through death into life. Be with me wherever I go, and with everyone I love. In Christ's name I ask it. Amen."

eight

St. Paul, or whoever it was, wrote to the Ephesians that he
always remembered them in his prayers, asking God, among
other things, to give them "a spirit of revelation in the knowledge of him," which is just about what you would expect him
to ask. But then he added an explanatory phrase that I for one
would not have expected and maybe for that reason never even
noticed until it jumped off the page at me the other day—
"having the eyes of your heart enlightened, that you may know
what is the hope to which he has called you." *The eyes of your
heart*, of course, is the phrase. "O altitudo!" as Sir Thomas
Browne would have said—to find such words where I never
found them before and just when I needed them. That day on
the staircase when I met my first grandchild for the first time,
what I saw with the eyes of my head was a very small boy with
silvery gold hair and eyes the color of blue denim coming down
toward me in his mother's arms. What I saw with the eyes of

my heart was a life that without a moment's hesitation I would have given my life for. To look through those eyes is to see every kingdom as magic.

"The hope to which he has called you" is what you will see with them, says Ephesians, and suddenly in this quiet, book-filled room where I sit with my feet up and a cup of tepid coffee at my elbow, everything I see with them speaks of that hope. On one of the shelves of American fiction there is a glass ball that snows inside when you shake it, the white flakes tumbling slowly down on Dorothy, who has been overcome by the deadly poppy field with Toto at her side and the faithful Tin Woodman standing beside her with one hand raised to his brow as he peers out for something to deliver her. With the eyes of his tin head he does not see that it is the snow itself that will do it by waking her up, as the movie has it. Or that it is he and the Scarecrow who will end up carrying her to safety, according to the book. Or that one way or another it is of course no less than L. Frank Baum, the wizard himself, who will see to it that in the long run nothing, not even the Wicked Witch and her legions, will be able to destroy these creatures whom he loves, because they are his and because it is in him that they live and move and have their being. He cannot see all this with the eyes of his heart because of course the wizard has not yet given him a heart.

Ganesh is nearby on the same shelf—Ganesh the debonair and gentle, Parvati's son and gate-keeper, whose head Siva lopped off in a fit of pique only to feel sorry afterwards and replace it with the head of an elephant. He is made of terracotta and sits pot-bellied and four-armed with his toys in his hands—an elephant goad, a string of beads, a bowl for alms, something that looks like a television remote control. His trunk is curled artfully just above his left breast, and his right leg is tucked under him. He has a kind of triple tiara on his head reminiscent of the one the pope wears on gala occasions. When he rides, he rides on a rat, which is small and cunning enough to thread its way through anything, and when he walks, he tramples all obstacles underfoot or uproots them with his trunk. He is the bestower of prosperity and well-being, and it is said that nothing should be begun, not even the worship of another god, without first honoring him. I honor him by asking his help in hoping for what I have seen with my heart.

I hope that it is true about God. I hope that it is true about Jesus. I hope that maybe it is true even that Jamie and I haven't seen the last of each other. He said "Ah-h-h" when I said it to him, the "Ah-h-h" you comfort a child with, or of being comforted by a child as I was not long ago by Dylan. We were in the hammock together, and when we finished reading *Ant and Bee and the Rainbow* for something like the hundred and fiftieth time, we lay there for a while just looking up through the trembling leaves to the topmost branches of the maples some sixty feet above our heads and decided that you would have to be a bird to get up there. Or an angel, Dylan said—he was four at the time—which turned our conversation in another direction. Someday he would be an angel himself, he said, and I said that would not be for a very, very long time. I would get to be an angel long before he did if I got to be one at all, I told him, but

I would wait for him, and then he said, "When I get there I will follow you wherever you go."

"Ah-h-h," I said.

When we were first married, Judy and I spent a couple of days with Jimmy in his house at 107 Water Street in Stonington, Connecticut. In the afternoon, we went swimming off a dock somewhere, and when I exclaimed with disgust as some slimy, seaweedy things on the bottom wrapped themselves around my feet, he said they were really quite nice when you got to know them and in fact would be joining us later for cocktails. A few years earlier I had unwittingly made a major contribution to American letters by giving him his first Ouija board as a birthday present. It was the Parker Brothers version that you can buy at toy stores, but once he got serious about it, I suggested that instead he should make a more authentic one out of a sheet of brown wrapping paper with the letters, numbers, and "Yes" and "No" crayoned on it, an upside-down teacup to serve as the planchette, and a sprinkling of talcum powder to ease its transit. A friend of mine named Dick Martin, once my English teacher at Lawrenceville and later my faculty colleague there, had just died, and I asked Jimmy if he thought that Ephraim, his major contact in the spirit world at that time, could possibly put us in touch with him. He said you could never tell about Ephraim but would give it a try, and then he took us into the dining room he described in a poem with its

Walls of ready-mixed matte "flame" (a witty
Shade, now watermelon, now sunburn).

Overhead, a turn of the century dome
Expressing white tin wreathes and fleurs-de-lys
In palpable relief to candlelight.

In almost no time he and his friend David Jackson had the teacup zigzagging over the powdered brown paper with such speed that it was all I could do, as the recorder, simply to write the letters down with no time until afterwards to see how they divided up into words. Ephraim, a first-century Jew who spoke resentfully about how his parents' marriage had been broken up when his father left home to become a follower of Jesus, seemed to know all there was to know about everyone's previous incarnations. My mother-in-law was a little disappointed, I think, to learn when I told her later that she had been no more than a nineteenth-century Greek guerrilla in some scuffle with the Turks, "a formidable woman," as Ephraim described her, who had given birth to some fourteen children. As for me, he said, I had been, if I remember rightly, an Ethiopian teacher of mathematics. Like the switchboard operator in some great hotel, he had no difficulty then in getting hold of Dick Martin, and from that point on the conversation was directly with him.

Although Jimmy had scarcely known him at school and David Jackson had never so much as heard his name, the voice that came through was unmistakably Dick's, and he gave a number of details about how he had died that neither of them had any way of knowing. He said, for instance, that he had lost consciousness at the dining room table and that as he was sitting there slumped over, he had realized that he had to make a life-and-death choice about whether or not ever to wake up again, adding that all of us have the same choice every time we go to sleep. I said to him then that he had never been a believer when he was alive, and I wondered if his views had changed, to which his reply was, "Have a better seat now." When I asked him what it was like wherever he was, he said, "Like Dante. Thank goodness there is no Act One." Was it possible, I continued, for him to describe in any way the look of the place, and letter by letter the teacup spelled out:

L-A-N-D-S-C-A-P-E-S-O-F-A-I-R

When years later I asked Jimmy if he thought it was really another world that he was in touch with or only his own subconscious, his answer was that he found it equally fascinating either way.

"Do you really believe anything *happens* after you die?" my mother asked me once in a suddenly hushed, intimate voice as if to reassure me that whatever I said would go no further. So when I got home, I wrote her the answer I couldn't shout and I suspect she never read. But now she knows the answer in a way that I cannot, who know only the hope that I see with the eyes of my heart. Is that hope anything more than an *ignis fatuus?* Either my mother knows that too or else she knows nothing at all because there is nothing of her left except what's in the cardboard box that I asked Jamie to be the one to place in the small, square hole in Irwin, Pennsylvania, thinking about how for so long he had been the one to do everything else she needed done. Does anything really *happen* after you die? How would she answer that now if Jimmy were still around to get hold of her on his Ouija board?

I know what my father would say because once he said it. At least maybe it was my father. I haven't played with a Ouija board for years because, Jimmy's experience notwithstanding, I have always found something dim and slightly unwholesome about it, but once a few years ago I tried writing out a dialogue between my father and me using my left hand, because the childish scrawl it produced seemed to put me in touch with the child I was when I knew him and—who can say?—maybe with him too. "I've been so worried. I've been so scared," my left hand wrote, and then he wrote back, "Don't be. There is nothing to worry about. That is the secret I never knew, but I know it now." I have the manuscript still, and it is so clumsily written that I can hardly make it out. "What do you know, Daddy?" it reads, and then his answer: "I know plenty, and it's all good."

If only Ganesh could clear the way for me with his great trunk, lend me his rat to find a path through the maze. Can it be true what I've seen with my heart's eyes? Can it be that what my father said is true, that in some sense it was truly my father who said it? Can it be true that Jamie and I have not seen the last of each other? His widow writes that she is haunted by the image of "his sweet head bowed in final release," and now I am haunted by it. I cannot bring myself to think of that image as the end of everything he was.

"Well, I can tell you that at least you haven't seen the last of me," Naya says, and it is true that I do all but see her. She is wearing a white linen dress that I remember from Tryon days, when she would sit out on the terrace in a wicker peacock chair with the Blue Ridge Mountains in the distance behind her. She is sitting now in a chair catty-cornered to mine in the library. On her right is the large triple window with Jimmy's head on the sill and various objects scattered around including the heart-shaped stone from Outer Farne. On her left is the fireplace with the tray John Kouwenhoven made me out of cigarette-box wrappers on the mantel.

"In answer to your mother's question, *I* have happened anyhow," she says.

Or is it only a vision of her that has happened, of how she looked all those years ago when everybody was alive still? Is it only a dream that I have conjured up, choosing words with great care to evoke her as best I can? I try to conjure up Jamie. Just for a moment he stands in the shadowy, inner part of the library at the opposite end from the large window, the part where the biographies are and the table with the double-headed brass lamp. He looks ruddy and fit in his khakis and a blue Brooks Brothers shirt with the sleeves rolled up. His head is tipped slightly back as if he is getting ready to laugh at something he seems to think I am getting ready to say.

"Why say *only* a vision, my poor ignorant child," she says, "*only* a dream—you of all people, with your religious turn of mind? Unlike you, I was never a great admirer of St. Paul. He always struck me as pig-headed and irascible in addition to being given to sentences so long and tangled that half the time I don't think even he was quite sure what he was getting at. But every once in a while, of course, he spoke with the tongue of angels—'What no eye has seen, nor ear heard, nor the heart of man conceived, what God has prepared for those who love him, God has revealed to us through'—well, through what if not through just such visions and dreams as you brush aside with your 'only'?"

I say, "I'm not just putting all those words in your mouth?" and she says, "No more, you might say, than I am putting them in yours."

The skirt of her white dress is dazzling with the sun on it, the upper part of it in shadow. How can I describe her face? It is mottled like the pages of an old book. Her hair is grey and parted just off center. When I was a child, Jamie and I used to watch how she would hold the comb first to her nose and then draw it slowly up her forehead till she found where the center was. Her eyes glisten under the folds of their lids, and she seems to be smiling at something that hasn't quite happened yet.

"What *has* he prepared for those who love him, then? I need to have you tell me," I say. "You know Jamie has died."

She turns her head slightly to look out the window. It is a bright, early fall morning. The leaves are still almost all of them green, but here and there you can see a spray of russet. Her sapphire ring glitters in the sun as she reaches out to touch the glass pane lightly with one finger.

"I used to knit black wool socks for him and get old Willy Westfield with the wen on the back of his neck to mail them off at the post office on his way home," she says. "He always told me they were the only ones he had that never wore out. He claimed his toenails made holes in all the others. I don't suppose he spent much time trimming them."

On the window sill there is a photograph of the two of us in a Plexiglas frame. We are standing on the beach in Florida in our bathing trunks. Jamie has a purple- and white-striped towel around his shoulders, and I am wearing some sort of white homespun shirt. My eyes are closed, and Jamie is looking at me. We are both of us laughing.

"I always thought that when you died, all things were made plain to you," she says. "I imagined that all at once you found yourself in the heavenly presence, and everything that had ever puzzled you was a puzzle no longer, and every doubt you ever had melted into thin air the way the Apocalypse says that every tear will be wiped from our eyes, and there will be neither sorrow, nor crying, nor pain anymore—those old words that are so lovely I could almost believe they were true as I used to sit there in Calvary Church hearing them read at some poor soul's funeral."

She turns from the window and faces me again. With her elbows on the arms of the chair, she has the fingertips of her two hands touching and is looking at me over them.

"What has he prepared for those who love him?" she says, repeating my question. "Things aren't the way I always believed they were. The mystery is not only a mystery still but deeper and grander than I ever supposed. It reminds me of how, when you're looking up at the sky, sometimes there's a break in the clouds and all of a sudden, lo and behold, you catch a glimpse through it of the real sky. The most I can tell you is that I think that it's we ourselves that he's preparing. Not just the ones who love him—how like that old sinner to leave out the opposition—but the ones who don't care a fig about him one way or the other."

"Then you don't see any more, wherever you are, than I do, wherever I am?" I ask. "No lamb on his throne? Everything is still through a glass darkly?"

"I have a better seat now," she says, and for a few moments the room is still. A cloud has passed over the sun, and the hills have gone a smoky blue. "I can just picture Jimmy bent over his Ouija board with his glasses sliding down his nose, concentrating the way he used to at the tinny little piano we had in that log cabin we rented one winter. It's not that I see more than you do, but that, from where I am now, I see farther, and the farther I see, the more I come to understand how much more there is to see beyond that. And your father was right, by the by, or was it your left hand? What you see can be a little frightening sometimes, and always more than a little overwhelming, but it's as good as he said it was. I would bet my bottom dollar on that." She draws her hands apart and holds them before her in the air for a moment or two before bringing them together again with a soft, decisive little clap. "It is as good as the sky is endless," she says. "It's as good as the sky is blue, and as fair."

"Landscapes of air," I say. "It sounds so empty."

"They are all here," she says. "They are here more than you are here now with me because they are more themselves now. They are more themselves than they ever were before. And when they are together, it is the way you and that little boy were together in the hammock the other day when you were looking up into the leaves with him and you suddenly felt very *émotioné*, less because of what he said than because of what as a child he was still able to be, what he helped you be for a moment with him."

"And Jamie?" I ask.

"Little by little Jamie will find himself, and little by little he will find all of us," she says. "And of course he will be found. No one is ever lost. Nothing is lost."

"Thank you," I say.

"My dear boy, you are more than welcome. I wish I'd been able to do better by you," she says. "I am a dream, but I am not only a dream. Will you remember that?"

I tell her I will remember that, and maybe I even will.

Is what she said anything like the truth? I don't mean a truth that I thought up on my own and then put into her mouth, but a truth, instead, that came to me out of God only knows where, the way Godric came to me once, and Leo Bebb, the way all my life moments have occasionally come to me when I said more than I knew and did better than I am. Who can tell?

Naya's answer to my mother's hushed, half-embarrassed question is that what happens after we die is that leg over leg, like that dog my grandfather was so fond of citing, we are off to Dover again. Dover is what God has prepared for us, she says, all of us, whether we love him or not—a Dover that, on this earthbound stretch of the road at least, no eye has seen, nor ear heard, nor heart conceived, and where we find our true selves at last and also the truth of each other and of the mystery at last. Has she any idea, I wonder, how much she sounds like her possibly least favorite saint? "Until we all attain to full maturity" is the way he puts it, and then those resounding anapests that I can't help believing she must have admired in spite of herself, "to the measure of the stature of the fullness of Christ," followed so quietly then by "speaking the truth in love, we are to grow up in every way into him."

Well, Amen and Amen is all I can say. Let it be true because I want it to be true. I feel in my bones that it is true. Sometimes I feel that it is beginning to be true, at least a little, even in me. As I grow older, less inhibited, dottier, I find it increasingly easy to move toward being who I truly am, let the chips fall where they may. I also find it easier to relate to others as they truly are too, which is at its heart, I suspect, rather a good deal like the rest of the human race including me. I find myself addressing people I hardly know as though I have known them always and taking the risk of saying things to them that, before I turned seventy, I wouldn't have dreamed of saying. Not long ago a young woman was here from Switzerland with Dinah and her family and because she seemed unhappy with herself somehow and unaware of how beautiful she was, I *told* her how beautiful she was. And at a church coffee hour of all things, after playing tickle-mouse with my grandson Tristan for a while to keep him occupied till his mother was ready to go home, I told an unknown woman standing nearby that there was a tickle-mouse on the loose so she had better watch her step, at which she gave every evidence, I thought, of being rather more pleased than otherwise by the prospect of possibly running into it herself. Years ago when I first started giving lectures and readings here and there, I rather dreaded the question-and-answer sessions that usually followed them, nervous that I wouldn't know what or how to respond and that the audience would see me for the impostor I more than half suspected I was. Now, on the other hand, it is the part of such junkets that I look forward to most, and I find myself responding to people I have never set eyes on before as though they are members of my own family.

The risk, of course, is that I will make a fool of myself, or worse, as I did at a jam-packed, deafening party not long ago when I heard myself telling the hostess that it was an insult to be asked to such a thing, because it had nothing whatever to do with real conviviality but was just a misguided way of paying off social debts, which everybody there would have jumped at the chance of writing off for the sake of being allowed to stay home. But it has been my experience that the risks are far outweighed by the rewards, chief of which is that when you speak to strangers as though they are friends, more often than not, if only for as long as the encounter lasts, they become friends, and if in the process they also think of you as a little peculiar, who cares? In fact it seems to me that I often feel freer to be myself in the company of stranger-friends than in the company of those with whom there is such a long tradition of reserve and circumspection that it is hard to transcend it. I feel closer to a man I know only as Rich and see only when I go to the post office where he works, and more nourished by the banter that passes between us, than is the case with many another whom I've known for years.

"Don't imagine, son, that these are things people need to know," are the words Jimmy imagined his mother saying in response to his sexual revelations, but it is in Jimmy's voice that I hear them now spoken to me, the same languidly modulated tone that he used when he referred to the first of my Noble lectures at Harvard, which he attended, as my "mad scene" and when, on being told that a certain poet and his wife were back in town as full of beans as ever, he said without skipping a beat, "Has-beans." These senescent *bêtises* of yours, I can hear him saying in the same voice. Wouldn't I do better not to bring them up at all as well as to exert myself never to make one again? That way I might be able to escape being reduced prematurely to a "character," a slippered pantaloon in holy orders—a *Presbyterian* pantaloon, he says. What he is thinking of, I suspect, are the far wilder risks he took with his own life by never in the slightest degree trying to seem like other people, not even as a child at Lawrenceville when the pressure to do so could be so brutal, but always remaining the Different Person, the Ugly, he knew himself to be, and by continuing to live as a practicing homosexual ("Practice makes perfect" I hear him say in that voice again) even after he knew the consequences could be fatal.

I think, by contrast, of how timorous I have been not only in my life but in these now four volumes of memoirs that I have written, in which I have touched from time to time on the dark guest who dwells in us all but have never risked laying fully bare the lust, the anger, the childishness, the paralyzing anxiety that are so helplessly part of who I am. "Only the young die good," the former dean of a great English cathedral wrote me at the time of Princess Diana's death. "We live by myths and fairy tales. What if Romeo in middle age becomes lecherous and corpulent and Juliet irritable and prone to migraines? I look in my mirror and see this raddled old cynic, duplicitous, hypocritical and selfish. And once I was a beautiful young priest. I could have been so remembered if I had died at thirty-nine."

I have never risked much in disclosing the little I have of the worst that I see in my mirror, and I have not been much more daring in disclosing the best. I have seen with the eyes of my heart the great hope to which he has called us, but out of some shyness or diffidence I rarely speak of it, and in my books I have tended to write about it for the most part only obliquely, hesitantly, ambiguously, for fear of losing the ear and straining the credulity of the readers to whom such hope seems just wishful thinking. For fear of overstating, I have tended especially in my nonfiction books to understate, because that seemed a more strategic way of reaching the people I would most like to reach who are the ones who more or less don't give religion the time of day. But maybe beneath that lies the fear that if I say too much about how again and again over the years I have experienced holiness—even here I find myself drawing back from saying God or Jesus—as a living, healing, saving presence in my life, then I risk being written off as some sort of embarrassment by most of the people I know and like.

For the most part it is only in my novels that I have allowed myself to speak unreservedly of what with the eyes of my heart I have seen. When old Godric makes out the face of Christ in the leaves of a tree and realizes that the lips are soundlessly speaking his name; when Antonio Parr has his vision of Christ as the Lone Ranger thundering on Silver across the lonely sage and then covers himself by adding that it may be only "a silvery trick of the failing light"; when Brendan as a scrawny, hollow-chested wreck of a boy sees angels spread out against the sky like a great wreath and hears their singing as the mercy of God; when every once in a while on even the warmest, most breath-less days Kenzie Maxwell feels a stirring of chill air about his nostrils or sees a snow-white bird circling around and around in the air over him as he takes his pre-breakfast walk on the golf course—they are all of them telling my story.

To that extent I have dared risk telling what I have experi-enced of God, but to live the kind of life that you would expect to flow from it passes beyond risk into a kind of holy reckless-ness that is beyond me. If it is true about God, then, as my father said, there is nothing to worry about, not even death, not even life, not even losing the ones you love most in the world because, as Naya told me, no one is ever really lost. If it is true, you would live out your days as one who continues to be afraid of many things, but in the deepest, most final sense is without fear. That is a level of faith beyond my reach, but at least once in my life I caught a glimpse of it.

I was flying somewhere one day when all of a sudden the plane ran into such a patch of turbulence that it started to heave and buck like a wild horse. As an uneasy flyer under even the best of circumstances, I was terrified that my hour had come, and then suddenly I wasn't. Two things, I remember, passed through my mind. One of them was the line from Deuteronomy "underneath are the everlasting arms," and for a few minutes I not only understood what it meant, but felt in my nethermost depths that without a shadow of a doubt it was true, that underneath, undergirding, transcending any disaster that could possibly happen, those arms would be there to save us if my worst fears were realized. And the other thing was a Buddhist metaphor that came back to me from somewhere. We are all of us like clay jars is the way I remembered it, and as time goes by, each jar gets cracked and broken and eventually crumbles away until there is not a single thing left of it except for the most important thing of all, the only thing about it that is ultimately so real that nothing on earth or heaven has the power even to touch it, let alone to destroy it, and that is the emptiness that the jar contained, which is one with the emptiness of all the other jars and with Emptiness itself. Nor is that Emptiness ever to be confused with nothingness, but is rather whatever of its many names we call it by—nirvana, satori, eternal life, the peace of God. Suddenly then, in that pitching plane some thirty thousand crazy feet up in the sky, I found myself not only not afraid of what was going on, but enormously enjoying it, half drunk on the knowledge that yes, it was true. There was nothing to worry about. There was no reason to fear. It was all of it, *all* of it, and forever and always, good.